Slightly n III

This book is dedicated to all who have served their country at RAF and RCAF Digby and its satellites.

First published in Great Britain in 2014
by Fox 3 Publishing
York
YO32 3QX (69)

Printed in Great Britain by
Inc Dot Design and Print
Inc Dot House
Seafire Close
Clifton Moor
York YO30 4UU

A catalogue record for this book is available from
The British Library

ISBN 978-0-9566319-3-0

Now I have heard the voices of the dead
I have read out the writing on the wall
And wearied out my brain upon the secret
And torn my mind against the jagged dark
And still I find no answer to it all!

Then it seems that I am doomed to extinction
And all my loves and hates will die with me.
No force is left to save me from this waste,
This careful shaping of a life in vain,
Which must, before it lives, find time to die!

The above poem was written by John Gillespie Magee,
when aged 16 years. It formed part of his poem
'Brave New World' and was written at Rugby School in 1939
for which he was awarded the Rupert Brooke Poetry Prize.
Rupert Brooke had been a pupil at Rugby School
thirty five years earlier.

Three years later at the height of war, whilst based at Digby,
he was killed in an aircraft accident flying a Spitfire.
He is buried in Scopwick Burial Ground.
Not long before he died he wrote the now famous poem
'High Flight'

An extract from High Flight .
The life and poetry of Pilot Officer John Gillespie Magee
by Roger Cole. ISBN 9 780957 116368

A Canadian pilot based at Digby takes some time out

Introduction

Near to most RAF stations, past and present, there are nominated burial sites for airmen and women who die in service. Some die in tragic circumstances, often in connection with flying. Others die from natural causes, road accidents and the like. Scopwick Church Burial Ground caters for nearby RAF Digby, near Lincoln. All that is seen by the casual observer are a number of neatly lined up gravestones showing just the name of the person buried and the date they died. Nothing is shown as to how that person lived their lives or how and even why they died and that is the reason for our book.

We have investigated each serviceman's death with the help of official records, published accounts, local enquiries and in some cases by talking with the families, friends and acquaintances of the deceased. We try to produce a well researched, accurate account of each one, whilst balancing the sensitivities of family, friends and sometimes the RAF itself. This particular book includes a large number of airmen of one of our Commonwealth allies, the Royal Canadian Air Force, who came over to the UK to help win World War Two only to remain forever, so many miles from their homeland. Each person buried at Scopwick Church Burial Ground has a story to tell. We hope you enjoy reading their stories and in that way they will never be forgotten.

Scopwick Church Burial Ground

A brief history of RAF Digby

This book concentrates on the people who are laid to rest in Scopwick Church Burial Ground rather than a formal and detailed history of RAF Digby. However in order to get a better understanding of the circumstances of the station and its people a brief history follows.

RAF Digby is said to be one of the RAF's oldest stations, being established on 28th March 1918, just three days prior to the birth of the Royal Air Force itself from its Royal Flying Corps roots. It was established on pasture land owned by the Earl of Londesborough with work commencing in 1917 to build the hangars, workshops and domestic accommodation. The airfield consisted of grass runways.

However, it did not set off in life as RAF Digby, but rather as RAF Scopwick, named as so many were after the nearby village. It was in July 1920, as the story goes, that too many spare aircraft parts were mistakenly being sent to RAF Shotwick in Flintshire that the station was re-named RAF Digby. Interestingly RAF Shotwick was also renamed and became RAF Sealand.

RAF Scopwick had its first experience of war when in 1918, just before the end of the First World War, a Zeppelin dropped bombs into a field about a mile from the station. This was not to be the last that RAF Digby, as it became, was to see of war.

RAF Scopwick opened as a satellite airfield for the nearby Royal Naval Air Station Cranwell and the Cadet College of HMS Daedelus which was shortly afterwards to become the Royal Air Force College, Cranwell following the formation of the Royal Air Force.

The station became an independent unit in November 1918 when 59 Training Station (Later renamed 59 Training Depot Station) moved in with the task of training officer and airmen aircrew to fly both bomber and fighter aircraft which included the Avro 504, Bristol FE2B and Handley Page 0/400 aircraft. The Station Commander at this time was Squadron Leader AT Harris AFC later to become better known as "Bomber Harris" the Air Officer Commanding in Chief of Bomber Command during World War Two.

Several squadrons came to Scopwick in 1919 staying only a short time flying mainly Sopwith Camels. Number 3 Flying Training School (3FTS) then took up residence from April 1920 until April 1922 when the station, having been re-named RAF Digby, entered a period of care and maintenance until the arrival of Number 2 Flying Training School (2FTS) in 1924. Interestingly, the station commander at that time was Wing Commander A W Tedder, later to become Marshal of the Royal Air Force, Lord Tedder.

Number 2 FTS stayed at RAF Digby for quite a few years, flying newer and better aircraft until a major re-organisation of the Royal Air Force resulted in the formation of Fighter Command on 13th August 1937. This saw RAF Digby become a part of 12 Group and by September 1937 two fighter squadrons, 46 and 73 had taken up residence with their Gloster Gauntlet, Gloster Gladiator and Hawker Hurricane aircraft. It was not long before both squadrons were fully equipped with Hurricanes and they were joined by 504 Squadron. It was also at this time that the 12 Group Lima Sector Operations Bunker was built on the station to control the fighter intercepts in the sector covering the North East of England and the Humber.

By 1938 war with Germany was drawing closer. Digby was allocated two satellite airfields at RAF Wellingore and RAF Coleby Grange with the Digby squadrons operating out of there. The first squadron scrambled from RAF Digby in the Second World War was 46 Squadron on 3rd September 1939 when there was thought to be an incoming raid, but the fighters failed to find a threat and returned to base.

View of the faithfully restored Lima Sector Operations Room Museum at RAF Digby.

Air Officer Commanding's Inspection of 46 Squadron 1938

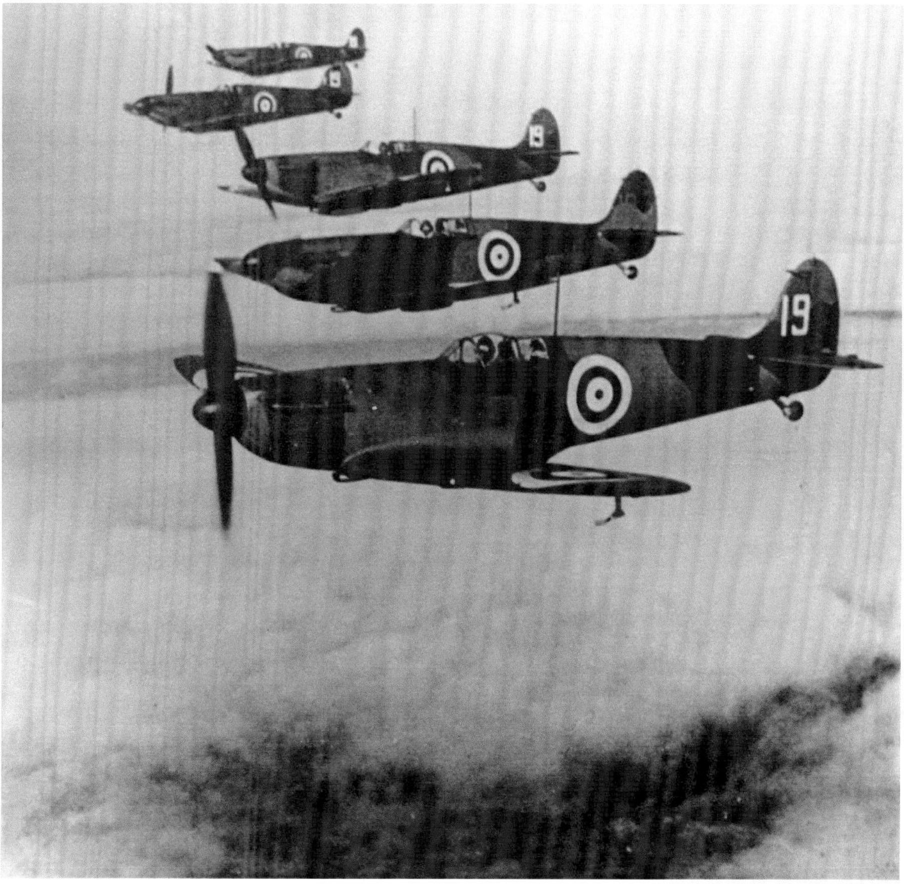

Spitfires of 611 Squadron 1940

In August 1939, 73 Squadron were tasked to form part of the Hurricane Wing of the Advanced Air Striking Force and flew to France as part of the British Expeditionary Force. For several months they were based out of forward French airfields flying many sorties over Le Havre, Louvres, Rheims and Verdun.

It was during this time that a much liked New Zealander, Flying Officer Edgar James 'Cobber' Kain became the first western air ace of the war. In eight months he had shot down seventeen German aircraft. He was awarded the Distinguished Flying Cross and was Mentioned in Dispatches. However, on June 7th 1940, the day he was due to return back to England, he decided to beat up the airfield on his departure in a war weary Hurricane. Sadly, following two low level passes he rolled the aircraft and was killed instantly when he misjudged his altitude and struck the ground. He was 21 years old.

Cobber Kain flying a Gloster Gladiator

On 17th June misfortune was to continue. With all the aircraft gone, the ground crew made their way to La Rochelle where they boarded the liner Lancastria for the passage back to England. Unfortunately it was bombed by enemy aircraft and sunk shortly after it left the port with a huge loss of life. Forty of the Digby based airmen perished

In October 1939 Digby was supplemented with the arrival of 611 Squadron who were flying Supermarine Spitfires and 229 Squadron flying the Bristol

Blenheim. The station became even busier with the further arrival of 44 Squadron and 144 Squadron, both flying the Handley Page Hampden light bomber and 29 Squadron flying the Bristol Blenheim. With 29 Squadron came the later to be famous Guy Gibson on his second tour at Digby having learnt to fly there in 1936 with 2FTS. Gibson was to earn the Victoria Cross in May 1943 when he led the crews of the specially modified Avro Lancaster bombers of 617 Squadron on the now famous "Dambuster" raids on the Mohne, Sorpe and Eder Dams in Germany.

Also in October 1939 two fighters of 46 Squadron saw action when, as part of a Digby based fighter screen, they attacked a formation of Heinkel 115 torpedo bombers attempting to attack a convoy in the Humber Estuary. Seven of the enemy bombers were shot down in all with the two pilots from 46 Squadron accounting for one each. His Majesty King George VI visited RAF Digby following this action. He presented decorations to several airmen.

His Majesty King George VI visits 46 Squadron crews at Digby on 21st October 1939 following their attacks on the German bombers

In May 1940, 46 Squadron were selected to join the Expeditionary Force, this time to Norway following the German invasion. Their aircraft were loaded onto the aircraft carrier HMS Glorious and on arrival in Norwegian waters were successfully launched from the carrier to operate on the mainland. After being involved in heavy fighting the unit withdrew to the carrier in June 1940 and managed to land on it despite not being fitted with arrester hooks.

12th May 1940. A 46 Squadron Hurricane at Aberdeen Docks waits to be loaded onto a coaster for onward ferrying to HMS Glorious out at sea.

The ground crew all reached the UK by other means, but sadly the aircraft carrier was attacked and sunk on 9th June. The squadron lost its aircraft and eight of the pilots. Only two of the squadron pilots survived. Although the squadron reformed at RAF Digby, within a few months they had moved south.

During the Battle of Britain in 1940, RAF Digby played host to members of many squadrons on rotational breaks from the intense fighting in Southern England. Among those to arrive was 222 Squadron from Duxford and the famous leg-less fighter ace Douglas Bader.

Squadron Leader Douglas Bader (4th from right) with members of 242 (Canadian) Squadron which he commanded from June 1940 immediately after leaving 222 Squadron.

In February 1941 the Royal Canadian Air Force arrived at Digby to commence their association with the station which was to last for the rest of the war. Number 1 (Canadian) Squadron and Number 2 (Canadian) Squadrons were immediately re-numbered to avoid confusion with RAF Squadrons to 401 and 402 Squadrons respectively. The Canadian Digby Wing was formed when 401 and 402 Squadrons were joined later by 409, 411 and 412 Squadrons.

Ground crew working on a Spitfire 1941

In November 1941 following several German bombing raids on RAF Digby there was a need to relocate the Sector Operations Room to the safer and more luxurious surroundings of Blankney Hall, a few miles away near Metheringham, where it was to stay for the rest of the war.

Above: Blankney Hall near Metheringham
Below: Various photographs of the inside of the Sector Operations Room

The Canadian Prime Minister with some of the crews

Group Captain Ernie McNab (Centre) outside Station HQ in 1943 with other senior colleagues

The Canadian Prime Minister, William Lyon MacKenzie King visited Digby on 8th September 1941, and spent time talking to the crews.

RAF Digby was fast becoming a very Canadian base and was re-named on 16th September 1942 as Royal Canadian Air Force Digby. It was placed under the command of an RCAF Station Commander, Group Captain Ernie McNab. In February 1943 the station received its first Mosquito aircraft which were allocated to 401 Squadron.

Numbers 288, 92, 609 and 198 Squadrons spent time at Digby during 1942 before the Canadian Squadrons 416, 430, 438, 441, 442 and 443 arrived over the next twelve months, staying generally until the early months of 1944. The station also played host to Czech, Polish and Belgian squadrons during this time as well as a handful of RAF squadron including the famous 617 Squadron between August 1943 and January 1944.

WAAF mechanics help a pilot to strap into a Spitfire IIA of 411 (Canadian) Squadron at RAF Digby in October 1941

Above: Refuelling a Spitfire
Below: Re-arming the aircraft

Aircrew back from a mission

By late 1943, early 1944 the station was being used as a night fighter unit and preparing for D Day operations. The latter was put into the hands of another famous fighter ace, Wing Commander Johnnie Johnson who took command of 144 Wing, consisting of 411, 442 and 443 Squadrons. Their purpose was to ensure air superiority for the D Day Landings and to move into ground attacking once the landings were established. Operation "Overlord" as the landings were known took most of the flying squadrons away from Digby.

The RAF Regiment then moved in for training following a re-organisation of their role.

Although flying from the station was greatly reduced there was an unusual incident on 16th November 1944 when thirty American Flying Fortresses which had been on a daylight raid over Germany were diverted into Digby. Many of the aircraft were damaged and needed repairs before returning to their home station in Norfolk, consequently they stayed for several weeks. This put great strain on the station's facilities, particularly as each aircraft had a crew of ten. It was not only the repairs that kept them at Digby, but bad weather and the bombers needing a particular strength and direction of wind to take off from the grass field. They still needed a fairly long take off run even though they would be lightly loaded.

By early 1945 the war was clearly coming to an end. The Canadians had returned to Digby and everyone was preparing for peace. By May 1945 the station name changed back to RAF Digby and the Canadians were homeward bound. On 22nd July 1945 RAF Digby left Fighter Command and was handed over to Technical Training Command. Initially under the control of Cranwell, a number of Technical Trade Training Schools arrived until they were relocated in 1953 and 399 Signals Unit took up residence on 1st October 1954, thus heralding a new life for RAF Digby. Subsequently army, navy and United States detachments joined the RAF in expanding the signals role as the Joint Service Signal Unit (JSSU) and the Aerial Erectors School took up residence. Renamed as the Joint Service Signals Wing (JSSW), Digby on 1st April 2005 it remains as such to this day.

The cemetery and the Cross of Sacrifice

The above picture shows the layout of Scopwick Church Burial Ground as seen on entering through the wooden gate pictured opposite. In the foreground left are the pre World War Two graves, beyond them on the left are three rows of Second World War graves with the occasional post war grave. The German burials are in a single row in the top right hand corner with a split row of mixed Second World War and post war graves forward of them towards the Cross of Sacrifice.

The Burial Ground was used extensively for those based at Digby and its satellites Wellingore and Coleby Grange. There are 71 military burials, being 26 Royal Air Force, 37 Royal Canadian Air Force, 1 Royal Australian Air Force, 1 Royal New Zealand Air Force, 1 Home Guard and 5 Germans.

One airman, Flight Lieutenant J H M Offenberg DFC, a Belgian national flying with the Royal Air Force, was repatriated to Belgium in September 1949. A marked flat stone signifies his original grave.

Cemeteries used for the burial of the military dead of World Wars One and Two are maintained by the Commonwealth War Graves Commission (CWGC) and Scopwick Church Burial Ground is no exception. However they do not maintain graves of serviceman who died outside of the war periods. A total of 52 of the graves fall under their jurisdiction, plus an arrangement to look after the five German graves. Regular grass cutting, setting of flowers in the borders as well as the upkeep of the grave markers are their responsibility.

In line with standard practice a Cross of Sacrifice is erected where CWGC burials exceed 40. The one at Scopwick Church Burial Ground was erected after the Second World War and officially dedicated along with the consecration of the grave yard on 1st June 1950 by the Lord Bishop of Lincoln. The Cross of Sacrifice, draped in the Union Flag, was unveiled by Air Commodore J L Hurley CBE RCAF. Air Commodore G R Beamish, Air Officer Commanding Cranwell Wing and Group Captain D Lumgair, the Station Commander at RAF Digby were also present. A Guard was formed by cadets from the Equipment and Secretarial Wing.

Service Burials and Grave Markers

Before World War One the burying of the deceased service man was traditionally the responsibility of the Ship or Regiment to which they belonged. No formal assistance was offered by what was then the Admiralty or War Office. Only a few that were buried in a military cemetery are maintained by what is now the Ministry of Defence (MOD)

During World War One there was no repatriation for those killed abroad and they were buried where they fell, or where they died in the various levels of medical care including those who were returned home seriously injured and then died. Such were the numbers of dead that the Imperial War Graves Commission (Later known as the Commonwealth War Graves Commission) was formed in 1917 by Royal Charter. They built cemeteries, designed by the best architects of the time all around the battlefields and on home soil. Bodies were laid to rest and graves were marked with a standard stone grave marker showing generally the crest of the Service or Regiment, the rank and name of the deceased and the date of death.

The relatives of those who died on home soil, often whilst training, in accidents or in hospitals from wounds, were offered service burials with similar headstones but possibly not such splendid settings of cemetery, or private family burial. Many First World War headstones for such burials can be found scattered in cemeteries or churchyards around the country. In between the First and Second World Wars responsibility for burials returned to how it had been before 1914.

During the Second World War the Imperial War Graves Commission again took on the role of recording the dead and maintaining their graves in perpetuity. Once again there was no repatriation and servicemen and women were buried where they fought and fell so they could be honoured together. Unlike the First World War, which was intense in particular areas with the high death toll producing large cemeteries, often quite close together, the Second World War was faster moving over land and featured many more casualties from airborne offensives. Where a World War One Imperial War Graves Cemetery existed near where a person died they would often be buried there. Others would be buried in new cemeteries built after the war.

Homeland burials, particularly those for RAF personnel, became quite complicated. Pre 1943 most RAF Stations had a local plot of land - often in a churchyard or local public cemetery where service personnel could be buried.

Whereas many families took the option offered of a private family burial at the deceased's home town, many others took the option of a Service burial.

Interestingly, where a member of aircrew died whilst involved in an air crash in England on the way to or from operations or in a training accident away from their home station and a service funeral was elected, they would mostly be buried at the RAF site nearest to where they crashed, as opposed to a return to home station. Many Commonwealth aircrew were killed in similar ways and were not repatriated to their own countries, but buried in exactly the same way, without the option of a family burial.

From 1943 with local cemeteries and burial places filling up, further burials tended to take place in large regional military cemeteries often near military hospitals. One example is Harrogate (Stonefall) Cemetery in Yorkshire, where 954 Second World War Air Force casualties are buried, around 75% of whom are Canadian. The Imperial War Graves Commission was responsible for the dead of both World Wars for an extended period after the end of the conflicts, to 31st August 1921 for the First World War and 31st December 1947 for the Second which allowed for those dying from injuries..

Airmen who were lost without trace, generally at sea, whether this be on operations or whilst training and therefore have no known grave, are commemorated on The Air Forces Memorial at Runnymede.

The Air Forces Memorial at Runnymede where the names of 20,315 RAF and Commonwealth Air Forces personnel who flew from bases in the UK and North and Western Europe are commemorated

From 1st January 1948, Ministry of Defence (MOD) policy was that if a member of the Armed Forces died in service, their next of kin would be offered a Service funeral and an official headstone to be maintained at public expense in perpetuity. However there was no repatriation for those who died outside of the United Kingdom, so they were buried locally or could be repatriated and buried at private expense with a private funeral.

In 1963 the policy of non repatriation changed. The next of kin of service personnel or accompanying dependants dying in North West Europe were offered either repatriation and burial at public expense or the cost of two relatives travelling to attend the funeral service overseas. In 1967 this changed to cover the rest of the world as well. The MOD maintain such graves and headstones of those who had a service funeral and a service headstone in perpetuity but where there was a private funeral or where the next of kin chose a non standard headstone following a service funeral, then the graves are maintained privately and the MOD has no responsibility for them.

Headstones are most easily identified by the shape of the top: Below left a standard Commonwealth War Graves Commission headstone with a simple domed top and right the standard post Second World War headstone with a "humped" dome top.

The following four pictures will help identify particular grave markers in Scopwick Church Burial Ground. Top left: one of the German grave markers. Top right: one of the privately buried mid wars grave markers, either crosses or engraved stone blocks. Bottom left: is a standard mid wars service burial grave marker. Bottom right: is the grave marker for the mid wars burial of Sergeant Bryce. Although there were slight variants in mid - war service markers, this is most likely to be a family grave marker produced by a local stonemason.

Scopwick Church Burial Ground

As you have read, the history of RAF Digby dates back to the First World War through to the present day. The cemetery at Scopwick Church reflects that history from 1930 up to July 1990. Many of the service burials are of airmen who died during the Second World War and seven are post that war. There are also eight burials of servicemen from the mid war years from 1930 up to 1936.

Details are shown of each burial in date order, headed by the name and rank of the individual and the date of death. What we have been able to learn about them, their lives and the circumstances of their death and others who may have died alongside them is shown in the text.

Pilot Officer Alfred Cecil Sant
Royal Air Force

Died 25th September 1930

Pilot Officer Sant was nearing the completion of his flying training at Number 2 Flying Training School, RAF Digby. Cecil had already completed three cross country flights and on Tuesday 23rd of September 1930 he set off for RAF Upper Heyford in a Bristol Fighter to complete the last one required before the award of his pilot's brevet.

The Bristol Fighter had been designed in 1916 by Frank Barnwell, whose son is also buried in this cemetery. Known as the Bris-Fit, the fighter first entered operational service at the Battle of Arras in 1917. The Bris-Fit's very first patrol met with disaster following an encounter with the Red Baron, in which four of the six aircraft sent up were shot down. Despite an unpromising start to its career, the aircraft eventually proved a great success and by 1930 it was serving as a training aircraft.

For Cecil, his cross country flight was not going as planned. Unsure of his position and with possible engine problems he landed in a field between Treeton and Aughton near Rotherham. After executing a safe landing he asked where he could find a telephone and was directed to a nearby colliery. He returned some time later having found out that he was about 30 miles off course and decided to set-off to Upper Heyford once again.

The aircraft took off normally, but was only 50 feet in the air when it suddenly began to bank and dived into the ground. Witnesses described how the engine did not appear to be working correctly just before the crash. It was later revealed at the inquest, that following a stop on the ground, such as this, the engine would have required fuel to be hand pumped into the carburettor. Flight Lieutenant White from RAF Digby, who gave the evidence, also surmised that it was quite possible that Cecil omitted to do this.

Bristol Fighter similar to the one involved in the crash

It would seem likely that just after take-off the engine failed; this may have been due to the engine problems he had been experiencing previously, or else fuel starvation caused by forgetting to prime the carburettor. In any case, once the engine had failed he allowed the air speed to decay which led to the subsequent stall. In an aircraft, a stall occurs when the airflow over the wing is reduced to such an extent that the wing stops producing enough lift to support the weight of the aircraft. Once this happens, in most aircraft, the nose will drop suddenly and there may also be a tendency for the aircraft to roll as one wing stalls slightly before the other and this is exactly what witnesses recalled seeing.

Following the crash, local colliery workers rushed to the scene where they found Cecil dazed and bleeding. The aircraft had hit the ground with such force that the engine was buried some way into the ground. Cecil was immediately taken to the pit's first aid post and later attended by the local doctor. He was then taken to Rotherham Hospital, where he sadly died on the 25th September.

At the inquest, Cecil's brother Martin expressed his family's thanks to all those who had tried to help his brother. The coroner replied:

"You will find they are all good men around here, Mr Sant. All the men in this colliery district are wishful to do their best for anybody in trouble".

The Sant family had already lost one of their own to flying. Cecil's eldest brother, Second Lieutenant Edward Medley Sant had died whilst serving with the Royal Flying Corps in France, when he was shot down after only eight days with his first operational squadron.

Flight Lieutenant Geoffrey M Shaw
Royal Air Force

Died 12th January 1931

The Vickers Vimy was an RAF heavy bomber which dated from the First World War. As well as an illustrious war record it achieved an immortal place in aviation history, when in June 1919 Alcock and Brown flew a Vimy across the Atlantic in the first ever non-stop crossing between St John's, Canada and Connemara in Ireland. By 1931, the Vimy had been relegated to training duties and it was in this role that it served with 2 Flying Training School at Digby.

On the 12th January a flight of three Vimy's were returning to Digby from Brooklands Aerodrome when the weather suddenly worsened. A fog had descended on Lincolnshire making it impossible for the flight lead, Flying Officer Bailey, to locate the airfield. He continued on, trying to identify ground features, but rapidly became more and more lost. As the short winter's day drew to a close it was quickly becoming dark and he made the decision that all three aircraft should land in the first available field.

Bailey made the first approach, but just moments from touchdown his aircraft hit a telegraph pole and crashed. Unbeknown to the airmen, they were in fact at Haxey near Gainsborough, many miles from Digby. Mr Fotherby, the Westwood Postman witnessed the first crash as Bailey encountered an unexpected obstacle:

"I was cycling along the Doncaster Road when I noticed the three machines manoeuvring. I surmised that they wanted to land, and it was apparent

from the continued hovering that the airman could not find a suitable landing place. There are many drains in this part of the country. I noticed the machines passing over the Park Drain Station. They were flying very low and I slackened my speed expecting them to swerve past me at any moment. One plane flew over the road about 30 yards ahead of me; it caught either the overhead wires or the telegraph pole, somersaulted and then crashed into a field. If I had continued at my usual speed it is possible that I should have been struck by the machine"

The Second Vimy in which Flight Lieutenant Shaw was a passenger made the next approach. Aircraftman Cecil James, the only survivor from this aircraft was able to give a vivid account of what happened next:

"I was in the cockpit, we were flying low in order to make a landing. We thought we could get onto a green field, but we over-shot and ran along the ground into a ploughed field and struck the bank of the Dyke. The plane shot up into the air and landed on its nose, smashing those in front. I escaped because I was sitting in the back."

When asked by the coroner what he felt was the cause of the accident, Cecil replied: *"We had received bad luck"*

The local doctor, Dr Marrison had been very quickly on the scene, but there was little he could do. Along with Shaw, Pilot Officer E M Chapman and Flight Sergeant Rogers had died instantaneously of serious head injuries, Miraculously Cecil had escaped almost completely unharmed.

A photograph of a Vimy aircraft from the archives of RAF Digby Museum. The position of the aircraft in a field, nose down in a ditch has similarities to this accident. Although we cannot say with any certainty, it may be the aircraft involved.

Having witnessed the first two aircraft crash, the third aircraft piloted by Sergeant Macmillan landed safely. He later reported:

"The crash occurred at 4:35pm on Monday evening, the light was bad at the time and darkness was falling. We were trying to get down before the visibility got worse"

Geoffrey Shaw was a 31 year-old Flying Instructor, originally from Scarborough in North Yorkshire. His Station Commander, Group Captain Smith was later to say of him: *"He had considerable experience and will be a great loss to the unit"*

Flying Officer Stewart Sinclair MacKay
Royal Air Force

Died 2nd May 1931

Flying Officer MacKay was attached to Number 2 Flying Training School at RAF Digby, where he had recently completed a course of instruction. It was a Saturday morning and he was the pilot of one of two aircraft flying at low level along the Lincoln to Sleaford road. The second aircraft was from Cranwell and flown by Flying Officer Southy, who witnessed the accident:

"I was about 100 feet above MacKay, following the Sleaford - Lincoln Road. He was turning on the level with insufficient banking and he stalled and crashed. Had he banked properly he would have got round"

This rather strange account of insufficient bank, may refer to trying to corner solely with the use of the rudder. It is possible that trying to turn by grossly over applying the rudder, may cause the aircraft to stall. In any case, the primary cause seems to have been low level flying.

The aircraft, described in the media as an Avro, crashed at Ashby-de-La-Launde, not far from the airfield at Digby. MacKay's passenger, Aircraftman Josiah Swain was on his first ever flight in an aircraft. He survived the crash and was well enough to leave hospital and give evidence at the inquest a few days later. Walking with a limp, he entered the courtroom, his head, left eye and right hand were heavily bandaged.

"We went up at about ten o'clock, I was in the rear cockpit. The last time I looked at the altitude indicator we were 1,000 feet up. We looped partly, righted, flew normal for a time and then did two or three turns. We rose again and the last thing I remember was going down again, I don't remember the actual accident. I scrambled out of the machine and went round to the front cockpit where MacKay was. I tried to get him out, but could only unfasten one strap. I said "Are you alright Sir?" but he only groaned. I took off my parachute and went for assistance."

The Coroner lamented the increasing number of aircraft he personally had seen flying at low level and recorded a verdict of death by misadventure.

Flying Officer MacKay has a private grave marker consisting of a stone cross mounted on an inscribed stone block. The inscription shows his date of death wrongly as 2nd May 1951. The reason for this is unknown.

Pilot Officer Adrian John Warford-Mein BA
Royal Air Force

Died 14th April 1932

Flying training has always carried an element of risk, indeed for many young men in the 1930's it was the element of danger and adventure that attracted them to a career as a pilot in the first place. Pilot Officer Warford-Mein was a 23 year-old who had ventured from his home in Australia to pursue his dream. His pilot training was progressing well having amassed over 50 hours in the air and an assessment by his instructor, Sergeant Sidney Trout, as having above average ability.

Once the basic art of flying has been mastered, there comes a time when every student must leave the comfort and safety of their home airfield and begin to practice cross-country flying. Adrian had practiced this flight a number of times with his instructor, but the 14th of April was to be his first solo cross-country flight.

Before taking-off for Bircham Newton at 11:45am, his instructor, Sergeant Trout ensured that he had plenty of fuel for the trip, he had also personally test flown the aircraft in the morning and he was happy that it was in perfect condition. The aircraft was an Avro Lynx bearing the registration K2352.

The Lynx was a derivative of the Avro 504 which had served with distinction as a fighter in World War One. Updated with a new engine it had become the RAF's primary training aircraft and was very highly regarded in this respect.

A little over an hour after take-off Adrian was in trouble, he was over East Winch near King's Lynn. Although Bircham Newton lies to the north east of King's Lynn, he had headed south east from the city. Two major roads lead out from King's Lynn, one to Bircham Newton and one to Swaffham. It looks likely that he had followed the wrong road and become lost. To make matters worse, a storm was brewing, it had started to rain and the wind had picked up noticeably.

Leslie Ruskin, an employee of Home Farm, East Winch witnessed what happened next:

"At about 1:30pm on Thursday afternoon, I was working in a meadow when I saw an aeroplane hovering over a field nearby. It circled three times as if looking for a landing place. It turned towards Ashwicken and then came round into the wind and dropped suddenly in a nose dive. I ran towards it and saw it crash."

Leslie rushed to the crash site, but although he could see the pilot trapped in the wreckage, the intense flames prevented him from making any type of rescue attempt. In any case, it was later established that Adrian had been killed on impact and he was already beyond any help. PC Tillett of Gayton, who was called to the crash site, later gave the following evidence to the coroner:

"I found the body in a sitting position with a parachute attached. This and the clothing fell away when touched. I also found a plate bearing the number K2352"

Due to the nature of Adrian's injuries, this plate became the sole means of identifying him, K2352 being the registration of the aircraft in which he was flying.

It will never be possible to know precisely what caused the accident, but a student lost in worsening weather is liable to make mistakes. It would seem that he became distracted and allowed the aircraft's speed to decay. Once the speed fell below a critical limit, the wing would cease to produce enough lift and would stall, the aircraft crashing to the ground in the manner described by the eye witness.

Flying Officer Edward Gordon Villiers BA
Royal Air Force

Died 19th June 1933

Flying Officer Villiers was the 22 year-old son of Rear Admiral Villiers from Hatfield Grange, Bishops Stortford. He had begun his flying training some four years earlier and had got off to a rocky start, with his instructor criticising him for '*Demonstrating considerable roughness with the controls.*'

However, he appears to have quickly overcome these problems and by 1933 was flying the Armstrong Whitworth Siskin, which up until the year before had been a frontline RAF fighter. Whilst at Digby, Edward was attached to Number 2 Flying Training School and on the 19th of June had been tasked with a machine gun practice at Donna Nook range near Mablethorpe. As he dived towards a target marked on the ground, he made an error of judgment and crashed.

This was to be the first fatal accident to occur at Donna Nook, an RAF range that remains in use to this day.

Armstrong Whitworth Siskin

Flying Officer George Edward Bullen Nixon
Royal Air Force

Pilot Officer Colin Kirkley
Royal Air Force

Died 18th March 1935

Nixon and Kirkley who were both New Zealanders, had taken up an Avro Tutor to practice aerobatics. The aircraft was fresh out of servicing, so should have been in A 1 condition. As they entered their second loop, something fell from the wing and the aircraft immediately fell from the sky out of control. The aircraft crashed on the farm of Mr George Flintham, who witnessed the accident:

"The plane was flying over Moor Wood at a height of about two thousand feet. I saw it loop the loop once and it was just soaring up on its back in the middle of a second loop when something fell from it and crashed into the wood. All at once the plane shot higher into the air then dropped to earth like a thunderbolt and buried its nose several feet into the ground"

Mr Flintham raced to the crash scene, but to no avail. Nixon was still in the cockpit, whilst Kirkley who had attempted to bale out was lying a few feet from the aircraft with a partially opened parachute. Both had been killed instantly. Two potato gangs had been working in adjacent fields and had a lucky escape when the aircraft crashed in the empty field separating them. Aerobatics can place additional stresses on an airframe and it is possible that the accident was caused by structural failure following excessive loading. It is also possible

Avro Tutor similar to the aircraft which crashed

that perhaps the recent maintenance had not been completed correctly. The enquiry never established why the piece, described as an automatic slot from the upper wing, detached from the aircraft, but verdicts of accidental death were reached for both victims.

A picture from an old local press cutting of the crash site

Squadron Leader Charles Robert Davidson MC
Royal Air Force

Died 21st May 1936

The inter-war years saw the British public captivated with all things aviation, even the art deco fashion of the day took its inspiration from the streamlined form of the new aircraft designs that were appearing almost daily. The usual routes towards becoming a pilot were either joining the Royal Air Force or else being exceptionally rich.

One Frenchman had a different view; he saw no reason why the average man on the street could not take to the air. Henri Mignet set about designing a small aeroplane that would be both affordable and within the capability of the average handyman to build. In 1934 he began to sell the plans to his new aircraft, the Flying Flea.

The Flying Flea was of unusual construction, with a tilting wing and a very large tail plane. The aim had been to make it easier to fly than a conventional aircraft. However, Mignet had unwittingly introduced some severe aerodynamic problems to his aircraft.

The Flying Flea ready for flight

Charles Davidson was an RAF Flying Instructor of some distinction, having won the Military Cross. When he decided that he would build a Flying Flea for display at the station's Empire Air Day, it is extremely unlikely that anyone would have worried about his ability to fly it. He started building the aircraft in February, and by May it was ready for test flying. Although there were problems with the engine stopping in flight, the test flights were thought to be going well. The engine, a Scott Squirrel, was sent back to the manufacturers for repair. With its return, all seemed set for a successful display at the Air Day.

Just two days before the display, Davidson decided to take the Flea up for one last test flight. The conditions were far from ideal, with a strong breeze blowing. He was even advised not to fly by Albert Leadbetter who had been helping him with the project. Davidson replied that he had spoken to other pilots who had been up earlier and they said the weather was fine.

It was a group of young schoolboys who saw what happened next. Sidney Price, whose father was an airman at Digby, had climbed some trees with his two friends to get a better view. He gave the following evidence to the inquest:

"The machine appeared to be in difficulty in the strong wind. It wobbled then crashed. The machine hit the ground the right way up, then bounced twice. It had crashed from a height of about a hundred feet"

The inquest was unable to determine the cause of the crash, but the coroner surmised that Davidson had been a little too keen to fly and had done so in unsuitable weather. In actual fact, the cause was a little more complex. All over the world, Flying Fleas were crashing at an alarming rate. In a number of countries they had already been banned. In less than two months, there had been three British fatalities all of which bore similar characteristics. In all cases, experienced pilots had just inexplicably dived into the ground.

The French Government ordered wind tunnel testing and it was found that the Flying Flea's unique design could prove fatal. In order to correct a small dive, the pilot would pull the stick back, which in turn caused the wing to tilt. As the wing tilted, it increased the airflow over the tail and thus increased the lift it was producing. The problem was that the tail was now effectively producing more lift than the wing and the tail rose, steepening the dive. The more the dive steepened, the more the pilot pulled back on the stick, compounding the problem.

These high profile accidents led to the demise of the aircraft for the masses and the craze for building Flying Fleas soon diminished. Today, there are still some examples to be found, but the notoriety of them is such that most pilots are still reluctant to fly them.

Charles Davidson had been the Chief Flying Instructor at Digby since it had reopened; he lived with his wife in Dorrington. His father was staying at the house at the time of the crash and he was vociferous in demanding an enquiry into the aircraft following his son's death.

The aircraft immediately after the accident

Sergeant John Bryce
Royal Air Force

Died 17th June 1936

Sergeant Bryce was 41 years old and lived in Married Quarters at RAF Digby. He died in the RAF Hospital at Cranwell from natural causes.

Flight Lieutenant Percy Don Walker
Royal Air Force

Died 29th November 1939

Percy Walker was an experienced pilot on 23 Squadron at Digby, but at the time 229 Squadron were in the process of reforming and becoming an operational fighter unit. To aid in the process, Percy was detailed to conduct an air-test on one of 229's Blenheims – L1452. Accompanying him for the test were two airman, Leading Aircraftman Chrystall and Aircraftman France.

Blenheim Mk 4 at Digby in 1941

Ben France had joined the Royal Air Force at the outbreak of war two months earlier and he was very nervous about undertaking his first flight. It is not known what caused the pilot to lose control of his aircraft, but it is possible that he was blinded by searchlights.

Percy ordered the crew to bale out, but only LAC Chrystall made it safely. The aircraft crashed at Owlet Plantation, Stockwith near Gainsborough, killing the two remaining occupants.

Flight Lieutenant Walker was buried at Scopwick, but Ben was buried in Sheffield, where it is said that the local laundries had to close because so many of the laundry girls wanted to attend his funeral.

Pilot Officer Walter Thomson Scott
Royal Air Force

Died 6th March 1940

46 Squadron had been operating Hurricanes from Digby since the outbreak of war. Despite initial success when the squadron shot down two Heinkel HE115s in October 1939, by March 1940 the Phoney War had settled in and little further action had been seen. On the night of 6th March, Scott was undertaking a night flying sortie in his Hurricane. At some point during the sortie his aircraft struck some trees and he was killed in the subsequent crash.

Pilot Officer John Sandes Barnwell
Royal Air Force

Died 19th June 1940

The Bristol Blenheim was the product of a challenge set to British industry by Lord Rothermere, owner of the Daily Mail, in 1934. At this time it was becoming evident that Britain was being left behind by the Germans in regards to aviation, Lord Rothermere wanted to redress this imbalance. His competition specified an aircraft that would carry at least 6 passengers and become the fastest aircraft in Europe

The winner was the Bristol Type 142 also known as Britain First. The aircraft was designed by the Bristol Aeroplane Company's Frank Barnwell and first came to the attention of the RAF when, during a test flight, it flew 30 mph faster than the RAF's latest fighter.

Naturally, the RAF saw the potential in this aircraft and from it was born the Bristol Blenheim in both fighter and bomber versions. Sadly, although the Blenheim was a massive leap forward for the RAF, it still did not match the machines possessed by the Luftwaffe and in the early years of the war Blenheim squadrons were to suffer some grievous losses.

On the night of 19th June 1940 Pilot Officer John Sandes Barnwell was flying a Blenheim IF of 29 Squadron, the very aircraft his father had designed. The Squadron had been detached to RAF Martlesham Heath in Suffolk where they were in the thick of the action.

At twenty five minutes past midnight, John and his gunner Sergeant Kenneth Long, had taken off to intercept an enemy raid. The Squadron's log records what happened next:

'After about an hour an engagement was witnessed over the aerodrome. The enemy aircraft was illuminated by searchlights and a fighter aircraft later established as Pilot Officer Barnwell's was seen at very close range. Fire was seen coming from Barnwell's front guns and the enemy's rear gun. The enemy's starboard engine was seen to catch fire and the aircraft went down out of control. Barnwell did not return after this engagement and although subsequent reports are conflicting, it is believed that he engaged two further aircraft. His parachute

was picked up from the sea on the following day and it must be assumed that he was shot down or crashed..'

Pilot Officer Barnwell's body was later recovered from the sea at Walton, near Clacton on Sea. Kenneth Long's body was never recovered and he is commemorated on the Runneymede Memorial.

The German Aircraft was a Heinkel He111 on a mission to attack the nearby bomber base at RAF Mildenhall in Suffolk. The aircraft crashed into the sea, near the Cork Sand Light at 01:25, killing all four crew: Hauptmann Hermann Prochnow, the Squadron Commander was buried at Sheerness. Oberfeldwebel Hermann Wojis's body was washed ashore in August and buried in Huisduinen Holland. Unteroffizier Franz Heyeres and Feldwebel Richard Bunk have no known graves.

Pilot Officer Barnwell's grave marker which lists the other members of his family who died.

John Barnwell was one of three brothers, who all joined the RAF. Graduating from the RAF College at Cranwell in the summer of 1939, he won the King's Medal for achieving the highest academic scores during the course. The Barnwell family paid a heavy price to aviation. In 1938 Frank Barnwell, the father and the designer of the Bristol Blenheim, lost his life at Filton near Bristol flying an aircraft of his own design. John's elder brother Richard lost his life flying a Whitley of 102 Squadron when it ditched off Aberdeen. His younger brother David was also killed flying a Hurricane of 607 Squadron in Malta. The bodies of both brothers were never recovered and they are commemorated on the Runnymede Memorial.

Pilot Officer Alan Blanchard Lawton
Royal Air Force

Died 19th June 1940

Alan Lawton was a member of 115 Squadron, a bomber unit flying the Vickers Wellington from RAF Marham. Alan was killed in a car crash.

Pilot Officer Peter Sisman
Royal Air Force

Died 1st July 1940

The 30th June saw the first daylight raid by the Germans, when a lone raider had flown in undetected and bombed the city of Hull. One of the sixteen high explosive bombs dropped struck a storage tank at the Saltend Oil Depot, the flames from which threatened to engulf the rest of the plant. Following the battle to fight the flames five George Medals were awarded for gallantry.

Later that same day, Peter Sisman was patrolling the night skies over Lincolnshire, his senses perhaps heightened by the recent German raid. Just after midnight, the downward recognition lights on his Blenheim failed. Conscious of the fact that this would now make him a legitimate target for the ground defences, operations controllers ordered him to land.

As he approached the base, Peter spotted an enemy aircraft and decided to pursue it. The 29 Squadron record book records what happened next:

'As Pilot Officer Sisman approached the base he reported on the R/T that he had sighted a bandit, and that he was going to investigate further. He then informed operations that he could not keep the bandit as he was being illuminated and dazzled by searchlights. He was then given a vector for base which he acknowledged. Shortly afterwards a crash and bomb explosions were reported and it was confirmed that L1374 had crashed and that Pilot Officer Sisman and Sergeant Reed had lost their lives. On striking the ground the aircraft caught fire and the bandit bombed the wreckage causing a direct hit which practically disintegrated the aircraft. It is considered that Sisman was held in the searchlight; became confused and lost control of his aircraft.'

Peter Sisman was buried at Scopwick and his Air Gunner, Sergeant Andrew Reed was returned home for burial at Blyth in Northumberland.

Pilot Officer Aston Maurice Cooper-Key
Royal Air Force

Died 24th July 1940

Pilot Officer Cooper-Key

Pilot Officer Cooper-Key joined the Royal Air Force in April 1938 at a time when a second European war was looking more and more likely. Aston progressed rapidly through his training and on 14th January 1939 he joined his first operational fighter unit, 23 Squadron at RAF Wittering. In July 1940 he was posted to 46 Squadron at RAF Digby just as the Battle of Britain was about to begin.

On Wednesday 24th July, just a few weeks into his new posting, Aston was tasked with anti-aircraft co-operation training over Derby. There was good reason for Derby to test its defences against air attack - the city was, and still is the home of the Rolls Royce's aero-engine factory.

As he flew over Derby, the engine of Hurricane P2685 began to fail. The Hurricane was powered by a Rolls Royce Merlin which in all likelihood had been built in the city below him. Witnesses reported the aircraft trailing black smoke as the engine spluttered. With few open spaces, it must have been with some relief that Aston spotted a possible landing site in the form of Sherwood Recreation Ground.

Wreckage alongside the railway line

As he lined up for a forced landing in the park, he spotted children playing and used the last of the aircraft's airspeed to avoid them. In performing this heroic act, he left no possibility of his own survival and the Hurricane crashed into a signal gantry on the railway embankment just outside Peartree Station, costing him his life.

At the time of his death, Aston was 21 years old, he had been educated at the Sherborne School in Dorset. He is now officially recognised as one of the casualties of the Battle of Britain.

Sergeant Douglas Owen Stanley
Royal New Zealand Air Force

Died 26th October 1940

Sgt Stanley

A native of New Zealand, Sergeant Stanley had been born on 12th July 1916 in Tirau on the North Island. In his youth he had been an enthusiastic member of the Scouts and had eventually become the Assistant Scoutmaster. In 1938 he paid for flying lessons and upon becoming a qualified pilot he joined the Civil Reserve of Pilots. This was a scheme whereby the New Zealand Government offered a subsidy for flying training if the applicant volunteered for subsequent service in the Royal New Zealand Air Force (RNZAF).

At the outbreak of war, Douglas joined the RNZAF and began his formal pilot training with the Air Force. Following the award of his pilot's wings, he embarked upon the RMS Rangitane bound for England. It was during this voyage that he met another pilot called Robert Holder and the two formed a close friendship. The ship departed on 12th July 1940 and it was nearly six weeks before it arrived in Liverpool.

From that point on, Douglas and Robert's training followed identical paths, through operational training on 6 OTU at Sutton Bridge to their eventual posting to 151 Squadron at Digby. Arriving at their first operational squadron in early October 1940, they found that it was converting into a night-fighter squadron, a role that its pilots did not relish. Group Captain Smith who was a Pilot Officer on the squadron at the time recalls:

"Early in October we were told that the Squadron was, in future, to specialise in night fighting. We all lacked night flying experience. For example,

I had 8.30 hrs in my logbook, J.W. Blair had about 15 and R.L Smith just over 20. At about this time the Air Ministry published the L.M.F. (Lack of Moral Fibre) Orders and Instructions. I remember, we all roared with laughter and we all said that these instructions described our attitude to night flying to a "T". We all declared ourselves to be L.M.F. and asked to be posted to No 11 Group Hurricane Squadrons. We were told not to be bloody silly and get on with it, and of course, that is what we did."

So it must have been with some trepidation that Sergeants Stanley and Holder, the Squadron's two newest pilots prepared their Hurricanes for a night flying detail at RAF Coleby Grange. Sergeant Stanley took off first, with Sergeant Holder lining up his aircraft on the runway behind him. Just 500 yards beyond the runway Stanley's aircraft crashed in a ball of flames in full view of his friend Robert. Although the fire crews fought valiantly and extracted Owen from the flames alive, he died soon after in Lincoln Hospital from severe burns.

Meanwhile, Robert was still in the cockpit of his Hurricane. He was asked by his Flight Commander if he wanted to continue, stressing that nobody would think any the less of him for not doing so. In the event he decided to carry on

A pilot readying for night fighter duties

and took-off in his Hurricane. Just moments later, Roberts's aircraft was seen to enter a steep left-hand turn and subsequently dived at high speed into the ground killing him, just 700 yards beyond his friends crash site.

Robert was returned to Bidford for burial. He had been born in Bidford-on-Avon in Worcestershire before emigrating to New Zealand to become a farming cadet. It is likely that his family remained in England and this may be the reason he was returned there for burial.

Douglas was buried at Scopwick, but is also commemorated in his homeland. On Achilles Point, Auckland, overlooking the harbour is a seat which bears the inscription: 'Presented to the Citizens of Auckland by Private J.E. (Ted) Scherer in memory of his friend, Sgt. Pilot Douglas O. Stanley of Matamata who lost his life in England 26 October 1940'

Sergeant Kenneth Edgecombe Markham
Royal Air Force

Died 13th January 1941

In World War II a fighter pilot needed both exceptional flying skill and to be a marksman who understood the principle of deflection shooting. When trying to hit a moving target, it is essential that you don't aim where the aircraft currently is, but where you assess it will be by the time your bullets reach it. Attaining this skill took a lot of practice, and the only way of ascertaining whether you had been successful was to replace the guns with a cine camera which started to film as the trigger was pressed.

On this day Sergeant Markham, flying Hurricane P3062 and Pilot Officer Harper, flying another Hurricane thought to be V6816 had been tasked with a cine gun practice. The air combat which took place between Ancaster and Grantham, suddenly went very wrong. Both aircraft collided, with the damage being so severe that both pilots were either killed by the impact or else left with insufficient time to escape their doomed aircraft.

One aircraft crashed at Lod Farm, Ancaster. The other crashed in the grounds of Belton House, Grantham. Pilot Officer Francis Harper, Kenneth's 46 Squadron colleague, was buried in Ipswich.

Flight Lieutenant Joseph Benedict Reynolds BA
Royal Canadian Air Force

Died 18th February 1941

Joseph Benedict Reynolds

On the morning of 18th February, Red Section of 401 Squadron were at readiness at RAF Driffield in East Yorkshire. It was a cold winter's day, completely overcast with a cloud base of only 500 feet, not the sort of day any pilot relishes. At around 11:00 Sector Control at RAF Church Fenton rang through to see if an interception of an enemy aircraft at 20,000ft was possible.

Joseph thought that it might be possible and after discussion with the Squadron Commander, Flight Lieutenant Christmas, decided that he would give it a go. At 11:35 Red Section were scrambled and ordered to patrol Bridlington, angels 20 (20,000 feet). Red Section was a flight of two Hurricanes, the second of which was flown by Flight Lieutenant Norris, who takes up the story:

"I was Red 2. We took off at 11:39 and started on a course towards Bridlington. After approximately 2 minutes we started to climb through the clouds. Cloud base at point of entry was 700 feet. We climbed to approximately 2000 feet in heavy cloud and it did not get any lighter. Red 1 apparently decided to come down and I heard him report that he had descended. At this time we were at 700 feet, just below the clouds, about 4 miles south west of Bridlington. Red 1 started a sharp turn which placed me behind. He then re-entered cloud before I could reform on his wing, this being the last sight I had of him."

Norris climbed his aircraft above the cloud and found a gap between layers at 4000 feet where he expected to find his leader. Seeing no sign of him, he decided to return to base. At about 11:50 Joseph's aircraft broke cloud in a dive of approximately 60 degrees and crashed into Bridlington Golf Course.

The cause of the accident was never established, but it was thought that icing conditions encountered in cloud could have been responsible. The aircraft's instruments are driven by air pressure; in particular the air speed indicator is reliant on the dynamic pressure of air fed to it through the pitot head. The pitot head is outside facing the aircraft's direction of travel and sends the airflow to the air speed indicator. If the pitot head had become blocked by ice, the pilot would see his airspeed start to decrease and being in cloud, with no other references, his natural response might have been to lower the nose to regain that airspeed. By the time he broke cloud in a steep dive and realised his mistake, he would have had no time to recover.

This was a time of upheaval for 401 Squadron, they had recently moved from Castletown to Driffield and by the end of the month they were due to move to Digby. Digby was already home to number 2 Canadian Squadron and it would seem to be for this reason that they decided that the burial should be at Scopwick rather than Driffield. Joseph's funeral was well attended by members of 401 Squadron, including his wingman Flight Lieutenant Norris.

Joseph Reynolds was born in Annaheim, Saskatchewan on 18th December 1914. His father was an Irish immigrant who had moved to Canada in 1908 to become a farmer. Before joining the RCAF in 1938 Joseph had gained a Bachelor of Arts degree at the University of Manitoba and later worked as an accountant for the Civil Service in Regina. His younger brother was killed in July 1942 when his Spitfire was shot down defending Malta. The Reynolds Peninsula in Saskatchewan is now named in their honour.

Flying Officer Hugh Morgan - Gray
Royal Air Force

Died 22nd February 1941

Flying Officer Morgan-Gray was a veteran of the Battle of Britain. On 3rd September 1940, whilst serving with 46 Squadron, his Hurricane was set alight whilst attacking a Dornier Do215. On this occasion, although wounded, he was able to successfully abandon his aircraft. Sadly his reprieve was to be all too short.

Hugh Morgan - Gray

Just over five months later he and Sergeant Hudson were the two pilots of 46 Squadron's Blue Section. Receiving orders to patrol Mablethorpe at 8000 feet, Morgan-Gray led his section of Hurricanes eastwards across the Lincolnshire Wolds. It is presumed that visibility was very poor as both aircraft flew into the high ground, without breaking formation. The wreckage of the aircraft were found at Cabourne Green Farm, Asterby.

Hugh's brother Christopher Morgan-Gray remembers his early life:

"My brother Hugh Morgan-Gray was known in the family as Peter. He was the son of Major Hugh Morgan-Gray RAMC and his wife Hilda May. He was born in London during 1919 after our father returned from service in East Africa during the First World War. In the 1920's Peter went to a private school in Harlow, Essex and his first job was with Union Cold Storage in London. This was only for a brief period until he could join the RAF and learn to fly, which he did at Debden in Gloster Gladiators. One of the pictures I carry in my head at this time is of father and Peter sitting on the floor in the sitting room at my father's practice in Braunstone going through the flying take off drill -Switch on, switch off, do nothing twice"

Hugh was married to Elizabeth Margaret Anna Massey, they had one daughter Jane Anne Morgan-Gray who tragically he never saw. Sergeant Cyril Hudson was buried in Birmingham.

Flying Officer Charles Paul Henderson
Royal Canadian Air Force

Died 25th March 1941

On the afternoon of the 25th Charles Henderson took up a 401 Squadron Hurricane to conduct an air test. The aim of the test would be to confirm that recent maintenance had been carried out correctly and that the aircraft was at the peak of performance. It is not known how far into the test he had got, but whilst at low level, the engine failed.

Charles Paul Henderson

With only moments to decide, Charles must have selected a field and tried to nurse his stricken aircraft into it. However, in doing so he allowed the aircraft's speed to decay and it stalled into a field about one mile north of RAF Digby. On impact, the Hurricane's petrol tanks exploded, killing the pilot instantly. Rescue crews arrived within 12 minutes, but Charles was beyond any help.

Charles had grown up in Toronto, the son of an Army Captain who had served in the First World War winning the Military Cross. Charles had been set on becoming a pilot from an early age, applying to join the RCAF as soon as he graduated from High School. In the event, he was called up two days before the outbreak of war.

Charles's flying training followed what was an unusual path for the time and drew much media attention. He was one of five pilots to be taught by a female flying instructor, Miss Helen Harrison and the first to go solo under her instruction. He also went on to become the youngest fighter pilot in 401 Squadron.

A few days later the funeral for Charles Paul Henderson took place at Scopwick Church Burial Ground and was attended by many of his squadron colleagues and other personnel from the station.

Miss Helen Harrison in the front seat instructing Charles Henderson

Leading Aircraftman James Ernest Owen
Royal Canadian Air Force

Died 14th April 1941

In civilian life James Owen had been a radio assembly man for the Marconi Company in Canada and the RCAF clearly decided that they should also exploit these talents when he decided to join the service. James was enlisted in the General Duties Branch, specialising in radio on 6th April 1940. From joining, his deployment was quite rapid and by 20th June 1940 he arrived in Liverpool and following further training was posted to 402 Squadron on 12th December 1940.

James was originally from Ireland, being born in Belfast on 14th December 1920. It would seem that his family had emigrated to Canada as he was living with them in Montreal, prior to joining the service. James's medical records describe him as 5 feet 5 inches tall, weighing 10 stone with a fair complexion and blonde hair.

At 13:29 on 14th April, the air raid warning sounded over Digby. Just 15 minutes later, a Junkers Ju88 dropped three 500Kg and one 250Kg bomb on the station. The bombs landed in a line between the local Post Office and the Sergeant's Mess, causing some minor damage to the Mess. Normally, this raid would have had only nuisance value. Unfortunately Aircraftman J E Tigh and his passenger, Leading Aircraftman Owen were driving a 402 Squadron lorry along that route. The explosions blew the lorry clear off the road, killing Owen and injuring the driver.

Digby did not stand idly by whilst they were attacked. Fourteen of the station's anti-aircraft guns opened fire on the raider, as well as many personnel with their own rifles. However, the raider escaped and at 13:50 the all clear was sounded.

Officers preparing for the funeral are shown opposite.

Flight Lieutenant George Gordon Hyde
Royal Canadian Air Force

Died 17th May 1941

Flt. Lt Hyde

George Hyde began his working life in 1933 as an Investment Dealer in Montreal, but was already showing a keen interest in becoming a pilot. Spending $281.35 of his own money, he gained his Private Pilot's Licence with the Montreal Light Aeroplane Club. On 1st of September 1938, he took his flying ambitions one step further and joined the RCAF.

After training, he was initially posted to 115 Squadron in Canada, but the outbreak of war saw him travel with 1 Canadian Fighter Squadron (later to become 401 Squadron) to England. Arriving in the midst of the Battle of Britain, George was thrown straight into action. On 31st August 1940, the day which was to see the RAF's worst losses of the battle, George took off from Northolt in his Hurricane to face the enemy.

Whilst in combat with the Luftwaffe's infamous Messerschmitt Bf109, George found himself on the wrong end of their attention and his Hurricane P2971 was shot down in flames over Staplehurst. Although injured, he managed to escape by parachute and what follows is the Hospital report of the incident:

'While on patrol August 31, 1940 Flying Officer Hyde's aircraft was hit by what is considered to be enemy canon fire and burst into flames immediately. He was struck by fragments of canon shell in the left leg, left scapular region and occipital region. He sustained burns of eyes, forehead. Left side of neck and under chin. Burns on left wrist and forearm. These burns were 2nd degree. After descending by parachute he was treated at an RE RAP near Tenterden, Kent and evacuated via a field ambulance to a British casualty clearing station at Benenden, Kent. After three days he was evacuated to No.15 Canadian General Hospital. Discharged from Hospital 7th September 1940.'

Following two weeks convalescence, George was keen to return to flying and sometime after October 1940 was posted to 402 Squadron. George was known as somewhat of a character, always full of fun and wearing a broad smile. He had acquired the nickname of Kewpie, but the meaning of this has been lost in the mists of time.

On 1st May 1941, George was promoted to the rank of Flight Lieutenant and on the 17th was the section leader of three Hurricanes tasked with an air display in support of Metheringham's War Weapons Week. North Kesteven Rural Council had set a goal of £60,000 to buy three new bombers. In fact they raised £190,000. Metheringham's contribution of £20,000 was raised through a myriad of events ranging from an ENSA concert party to a baby show.

George had briefed his section carefully. They were to approach the village in Vic formation, that is one aircraft on the left and slightly behind George with the other aircraft in a similar position on the right. On his word, the two wing men, Flying Officer Saint-Pierre and Pilot Officer Walker, were to break away from his aircraft. George would then pull up, perform a half roll and return low over the village.

The fly past seemed to be going well, the Vic of three aircraft dived very low over the village and the two wing men broke away just as instructed. George pitched his aircraft up and climbed to a height of about 1000 feet and rolled inverted. His aim was to pull back on the stick and perform a half loop to return over the village. However, he had insufficient height to achieve this and his aircraft struck the ground at a 45 degree angle at very high speed. George was killed instantly by the impact. The Hurricane had crashed in a potato field between Kirkby Green and Rowston, known locally as the Pastures. Today, the track leading to the field is lined with Canadian Maple trees. Whether they are there by coincidence, or not, there can be no more fitting tribute to a young Canadian who gave his life all those years ago.

Briefing with other pilots - George Hyde is second from the left.

The funeral of Flight Lieutenant Hyde - buried with Full Military Honours. Below a Bugler plays the Last Post

Officers and NCOs around the graveside as the firing party perform the gun salute

Leading Aircraftman Edward John Lewis
Royal Canadian Air Force

Died 7th June 1941

The risks of combat are obvious, but it is important to remember that the servicemen of World War II were not immune to accidents of a more routine nature. For Aircraftman Lewis, the offer of a ride home, as the pillion passenger on a motorbike may well have seemed like an attractive offer. The motorbike was being ridden by Leading Aircraftman Geraghty and as the pair rounded a blind corner on the road between Wellingore Airfield and Wellingore Hall, they struck an RAF truck travelling in the opposite direction.

At the inquest, fault for the accident was never established, with each driver blaming the other. Although it will never be known precisely what happened, each drivers account of the accident follows:

"I am Leading Aircraftman Allen Wild in the Royal Air Force stationed at Digby. At 2pm on 2nd June 1941 I was driving a RAF Commer 15 Cwt van from Wellingore Hall towards Wellingore Heath. I had gone 200 yards from the Hall and was approaching a right hand bend. When 20 yards from the bend I saw a motorcycle approaching from the opposite direction. I was on my left hand side and very close to the kerb travelling at about 20mph (I had just changed into top gear).

The motorcycle came round the bend on its proper side at the beginning and then made a wide sweep well on to the crown of the road. I estimate his speed at 40mph. He tried to swerve out of my way. I tried to get out of his way and caught my near side front wheel on the kerb which is very high. The motor cycle caught the offside of my van just behind the door of the driver's cab."

"I am Leading Aircraftman Joseph Geraghty of the Royal Canadian Air Force stationed at Wellingore. On 2nd June 1941 about 2pm I was driving a motorcycle from Wellingore aerodrome to Wellingore Hall, LAC Lewis was riding as pillion. I know the road quite well.

When I was going round a left hand bend I saw a truck coming towards me. He was on his wrong side. I was on my correct side about 2 feet from the kerb. I imagine I was driving about 25mph and the speed of the truck was about the same. As soon as I saw the truck I put on my brakes and tried to pass but I hit the side of the truck"

On the day of the accident, this would have seemed like a minor mishap, with the only injury being a quite deep laceration to Edward's knee. On admission to the RAF Hospital at Rauceby, it was found that he had suffered quite bad damage to his knee.

Apart from mild shock, the only other injury was the contamination of the wound by dirt from the road. It was however this contamination that was to prove the fatal injury.

Over the next couple of days, Edward developed Gas Gangrene which is a bacterial infection that produces gas in the muscle tissues. It does not respond to antibiotics and the usual treatment can involve amputation of the affected limb. In Edward's case, amputation was not practical as the infection had already spread too far up his leg. At 1:20 am on 7th June he succumbed to his injuries. Edward was 25 and originally from Toronto, where he had been a truck driver in civilian life.

The funeral of LAC Lewis. Buried with Full Military Honours

Aircraftman 1st Class William Franklin Kidd
Royal Canadian Air Force

Died 3rd July 1941

Aircraftman 1 W F Kidd

William Kidd, originally from Franktown Ontario, had joined the RCAF to be a wireless mechanic and had arrived in England in April 1941.

On 3rd July 1941, having been on 401 Squadron for just three months, he boarded Blenheim Z5870 bound for Ringway near Manchester. Once there, the aircraft would undergo scheduled maintenance and the occupants would have the opportunity to take some of their leave. His fellow passenger Aircraftman Raymond Place lived in Manchester and it is likely that he was simply getting a lift home. William and the final passenger Aircraftman Cottam, may have simply taken the opportunity to go flying or else had decided to explore Manchester during their time off.

The aircraft, belonging to 12 Group Anti Aircraft Co-operation Unit, was piloted by Sergeant Nikodem 'Nikky' Plotek. It never arrived at Ringway and was only found when a local soldier, Gunner Hamer, stumbled upon the crash site whilst out for a walk. The Blenheim had come down, near to Lee Farm on Crowden Tower in the Peak District killing all on board.

Sergeant Robert Matheson Murray
Royal Canadian Air Force

Died 29th July 1941

Before the Japanese attacked Pearl Harbour, bringing the United States into the war on 7th December 1941, a common route for young American men to join the war in Europe was via the RCAF. Robert Murray was from Michigan where he had been a sheep buyer in a stockyard. Giving up his job, he travelled to Canada and joined the RCAF on 25th September 1940.

He completed his basic flying training in Canada before moving to England to complete the final elements at 53 Operational Training Unit. On 26th July, he was posted to the newly formed 411 Squadron at Digby and just two days later he was airborne in Spitfire P7755. It was a formation practice flight where Robert would be the wingman to Red Leader, radio call sign Red Two. These flights were a common introduction to flying on a combat fighter squadron and should have presented Robert with few problems.

Unfortunately, misty conditions meant that he lost sight of his leader and the aircraft was last seen by ground observers, flying at low level. At 13:20 the Spitfire crashed at Pyewipe Mud flats near Great Coates, South of Grimsby. The aircraft had buried itself deeply in the mud, killing Robert instantly. He was buried at Scopwick three days later.

Sergeant Raymond George Smith
Royal Canadian Air Force

Died 2nd August 1941

As the war progressed, the training system for pilots become more and more efficient, both out of necessity and the fact that they were becoming more proficient as a training organisation. Sergeant Smith's record of service gives a good indication of just how quickly a civilian could be transformed into a fully qualified Spitfire pilot. Joining the RCAF on 17th June 1940, basic recruit training commenced almost immediately, lasting just over two months.

Following a short period of leave, Raymond began flying training on 22nd October 1940 and was a fully qualified pilot by 18th March 1941 when he embarked for England.

All pilots trained overseas were first posted to a Pilot Reception Centre (PRC) and in this case, it was 3 PRC in Bournemouth. Hotels for peacetime holiday makers had been transformed into huge barracks for newly trained aircrew. Whilst at the PRC, Raymond would have received orientation briefings, flying equipment and generally kept gainfully employed until a place became available on his next flying course.

Having spent only 11 days at the PRC, Sergeant Smith was posted to 58 Operational Training Unit (OTU) at Grangemouth on 12th May 1941. The function of an OTU was to train a qualified pilot to use his aircraft as a weapon of war. Dog-fighting and aerial gunnery were key skills a fighter pilot would need before arriving on his first operational squadron.

On 23rd June 1941, Raymond arrived at RAF Wellingore, to join 412 Squadron as a fully qualified fighter pilot, despite most squadrons insisting on a period of their own work-up training. Bitter experience gained in the Battle of Britain had shown that throwing newly qualified pilots straight into combat was little more than suicidal.

On 2nd August 1941, just over one year since joining the RCAF, Sergeant Smith was airborne on a training sortie. The accident report gives a vivid account of what happened next:

'*Sergeant C S Maclean and Sergeant R G Smith, both of No 412 (RCAF) Squadron took off from Wellingore in Spitfire R7197 and Spitfire H4176 respectively. Combat practice had been authorised at 15,000ft, and the pilots had discussed the action to be taken prior to taking off.*

At 17,000ft, Sergeant Maclean signalled to break formation and commence combat. Sergeant Smith got on his tail and he changed to fine pitch and throttled right back easing the control column back to decrease speed. Sergeant Smith's aircraft began to overshoot underneath. A collision occurred, due to the lower aircraft pulling up while directly below, damaging Sergeant Maclean's main plane and airscrew. Sergeant Smith's aircraft showed in front for a second without tail assembly. (Examination after the crash revealed that the fuselage had been completely severed approximately four feet behind the cockpit, presumably by the other aircraft's airscrew).

Sergeant Smith's aircraft crashed at Silk Willoughby, south of Sleaford at approximately 1025 hours, the pilot being killed. As Sergeant Smith apparently made no attempt to bale out, it was probable he had been rendered unconscious by the collision.

After the collision, which occurred at approximately 9,200 feet, Sergeant Maclean tested his controls and found them all working. He received a homing and landed safely at base without flaps. It was considered that Sergeant Maclean acted with great coolness under the circumstances and was particularly wise in not lowering his flaps, as it was afterwards proved that had he attempted to do so, the starboard flap only would have operated which might have resulted in loss of control of the aircraft near the ground.'

Raymond was from Chatham, Ontario where he had been a Stockman for FW Woolworth and later the Deputy Manager of a Five and Ten Cent store. He was married to Betty Jane, but they had no children.

Pilot Officer William Robert Hughes
Royal Canadian Air Force

Died 31st August 1941

In the crowded skies of wartime Lincolnshire even a routine mission held its dangers. As the 44 Squadron Hampden lined up for take-off at Waddington, its pilot, Pilot Officer Owen could hardly have realised that just moments later he and his entire crew would be dead. As Hampden AD939 climbed away from the airfield heading south, it collided with a Spitfire of 412(Falcon) Squadron from nearby RAF Digby.

William was the pilot of the Spitfire AD8586. He had joined the squadron only five days earlier and was up on a training flight. He had been airborne for 45 minutes in what were later described as rather hazy conditions. Whilst over Waddington, his aircraft collided with the Hampden, causing both aircraft to immediately dive into the ground, killing both crews instantly.

Before joining the RCAF, William had been a Clerk at the Royal Bank of Canada in Ontario. He was unmarried and was 25 years old at the time of his death.

A Hampden of 44 Squadron at Waddington

Wing Commander Norman Bredsgaard Petersen
Royal Canadian Air Force

Died 2nd September 1941

Wing Commander Petersen

Wing Commander Petersen was a career pilot, who had joined the RCAF in June 1931. Before the war he had been a flying instructor, and was instrumental in the training of other flying instructors for the Central Flying School. At the outbreak of war he was appointed the Chief Flying Instructor of the Central Flying School in Trenton Ontario, later becoming its commanding officer. For this work, he was later recommended for the award of the Air Force Cross and although the Air Officer Commanding was in agreement, he did not feel that he should make the award posthumously.

In May 1941 he left Canada to take command of 409 Squadron, which at the time was flying the Boston Paul Defiant. The Defiant had been designed as a day fighter and unusually for an aircraft of this type carried a powered machine gun turret. It had proved very disappointing as a day fighter and had been relegated to night fighter duties, not because it was particularly well suited to this role, but for want of anything better.

Petersen had his reservations about the Defiant, but got his squadron into shape and within a month he had them operational at RAF Coleby Grange.

On the 28th August the squadron were finally equipped with a more potent aircraft, the twin-engine Bristol Beaufighter. Just a few days later, Norman was flying a familiarisation sortie on the Beaufighter together with the squadron Signals Officer Pilot Officer Slater RAF. It would seem that a slight bounce on take-off had damaged the undercarriage. Petersen reported on the radio that he was unable to get the undercarriage to lock down and that he was going to make an approach. His aim would most probably have been to allow the aircraft to roll along the runway to test the undercarriage whilst still having enough power to stop it fully collapsing if it was not locked.

Applying full power, he took-off again and made a circuit of the airfield, but just over a mile from touchdown, the aircraft crashed. There were several witnesses to the crash including two civilian girls who were less than 100 yards from the crash scene:

'*The evidence of all these witnesses is very consistent; they all agree that the Beaufighter was seen to be making a left-hand turn and then to straighten out and suddenly flick over towards the right. The flick over carried it over the vertical and the aeroplane finally ended up on its back. The evidence indicates that the height could not have been more than 100 feet*'.

The investigation concentrated on the fact that Petersen was extremely low for that phase of landing, being over a mile from the airfield. It was thought that he may have become distracted by his undercarriage problems and allowed his speed and height to decrease. Indeed, the witnesses describe the classic entry to a spin. A plausible train of events is that whilst distracted by the undercarriage, he descended too low and upon suddenly realising his predicament, he pulled back on the stick and applied power. Because the engines take time to respond, combined with an already low airspeed, a spin was highly probable. The aircraft was far too low to recover from the spin or for any chance of escape and both occupants were killed instantly.

Norman's death was a grievous loss to the squadron and they had a great deal of difficulty reconciling such an accident with a pilot who was renowned for his skill and coolness under pressure. The only explanation the Station Commander, Group Captain A P Campbell, could offer was as follows:

"*He was such a level headed and careful pilot and the last man to get flustered. It is possible, however, that he was worried about the fact that he, as Commanding Officer, was going to be forced to crash the first Beaufighter on the aerodrome through having to make a landing with a collapsed undercarriage.*"

Norman in flying kit

The funeral of Wing Commander Petersen was very well attended by both squadron and station personnel as each of these pictures show.

Flight Lieutenant Frederick Stanley Watson
Royal Canadian Air Force

Died 11th October 1941

The Boulton Paul Defiant was quite a revolutionary aircraft, combining the manoeuvrability and speed of a single seat fighter, with the firepower of a rear facing powered machine gun turret. In the early days of the war it proved quite successful. Its similarity in appearance to the Hurricane perhaps led German fighter pilots to believe they could safely attack it from the stern. Anybody foolish enough to do so would experience unexpected and quite devastating defensive fire from the Defiant.

By the time of the Battle of Britain, the Germans had become wise to this aircraft, exploiting the fact that it had no forward firing guns and was also vulnerable to attack from below. The Defiant soon began to take unsustainable losses in the day-fighter role and was soon relegated to night-fighter duties. In this role it was to prove quite successful.

Equipped with the Defiant, 409 Squadron RCAF were based at Coleby Grange, just South of Lincoln where they were tasked with defending the night skies over East Anglia. Watson and his Air Gunner, Flight Sergeant McKinnon were on a routine patrol over Norfolk, when Watson made a radio call to say his flying instruments had failed. He immediately ordered the Air Gunner to bale out, but before he could do the same, his aircraft entered a cloud bank, where he lost control. Watson was killed when the aircraft crashed at Wolverton near Sandringham. Fortunately McKinnon had baled out in time and survived without injury.

The Boulton Paul Defiant

Frederick Watson was married with a four year old son. He was originally from Winnipeg, Manitoba, where he had worked as an Advertising Manager. He was also a veteran of the Battle of Britain, having flown with 3 Squadron during the conflict.

Sergeant Norman Allan Ritchie
Royal Canadian Air Force

Died 22nd November 1941

Sergeant Ritchie

Norman who was known to his family as Bud, was the eldest of three children to a Canadian father and American mother. Born in Regina, Saskatchewan, he was living in Edmonton at the time he joined the Royal Canadian Air Force on 19th October 1940. Norman was amongst the first of his countrymen to sign up to fight the war in Europe, which was entirely in line with the strong sense of duty he had developed in his early years.

Norman's sister Betty describes her early life with her brother: *"Bud was a year older than me, but he loved the outdoors and always took me everywhere with him. He didn't treat me like "just a girl", teaching me to climb trees, ride horseback and other things which were not things most girls did at that time. He looked after me and taught me that everyone was equal. He was very gentle and treated everyone equally. What stands out is that he had a black man as a friend and fellow musician in his band at a time when there was an extreme colour differentiation between the races. He was exceptionally smart and loved to teach others, especially his younger brother and sister."*

In civilian life, Norman had been an accomplished musician and had his own band, which played in the Alberta area. During his selection interview for the RCAF, he was described as a clean cut, cool and likeable chap and was recommended for training as a pilot. By August 1941 he had completed his basic flying training and was shipped to the United Kingdom to complete his operational training. Before leaving, he had become engaged to be married, but just a few months later he would die in a flying accident at Digby.

On 21st November 1941, Norman was flying a Westland Lysander II (P1714) of 12 Group AA Flight. The weather at Digby was very poor and Norman had only 6 hours and 15 minutes experience flying a Lysander. It is thought that he became disconcerted by the bad weather and attempted to land down-wind. Upon realising his error, he opened up the throttle and attempted to go around for another approach. Unfortunately in doing so he allowed the aircraft to climb too steeply and it stalled into the ground. Both Norman and his passenger Sergeant J F Stein were badly injured and were rushed to the nearby

Norman in scout uniform with his mother and siblings in 1928

RAF Hospital at Rauceby. Sadly, Norman succumbed to his injuries the next day, but records indicate that Sergeant Stein went on to survive the war.

As this was occurring, his sister Betty was at Halifax University and recalls a strange experience:

"I vividly remember waking in the night from a very vivid dream about someone in a hospital bed trying to reach me about my brother. I was very upset by the dream and finally went back to sleep. It was the following day that we received news that Bud had died that night."

On hearing the terrible news, Norman's younger brother Robert, immediately went out to enlist in the RCAF. Robert went on to become a pilot like his brother and as well as serving through the war he continued into a professional career in the post-war RCAF. Robert became a Search and Rescue pilot and was honoured for saving many lives. Betty became Canada's first female Queen's Council and is a holder of the Order of Canada and Queen's Diamond Jubilee Medal for her work on human rights. It is testament to the character of this man's short life that she attributes her values to the lessons he taught her as a young child.

Norman in training

Norman on right with younger brother Robert

A Lysander as flown by Sergeant Ritchie

Pilot Officer John Gillespie Magee
Royal Canadian Air Force

Died 11th December 1941

John Gillespie Magee

John Gillespie Magee first became well known as a poet, when President Ronald Reagan used words from his poem "High Flight" in an address to the American people, following the 1982 Challenger disaster which included:

"We will never forget them, nor the last time we saw them, this morning, as they prepared for their journey and waved goodbye and ***"slipped the surly bonds of Earth to touch the face of God"***

The inspiration for the poem had come to John whilst conducting a high altitude test flight of a Spitfire V on 3rd September 1941. Once on the ground, he completed the poem and sent a copy of it to his parents with the following words:

"I am enclosing a verse I wrote the other day. It started at 30,000ft and was finished soon after I landed. I thought it might interest you."

John was born in Shanghai on 9th June 1922, where his parents were missionaries. Growing up in China, he became a fluent Chinese speaker, but by the age of nine his parents felt the time was right for him to continue his education in England. Attending the illustrious Rugby School, his aptitude for poetry came to the fore, winning the school's poetry prize, a prize which had been named after the renowned First World War poet and former Rugby School pupil, Rupert Brooke.

Although he was born in China, John was in fact an American citizen and in 1939 he left England to continue his education in the United States, eventually winning a scholarship to study Classics at Yale. Before John could take up that scholarship and with the Battle of Britain at its height, he felt the calling to fight fascism.

After deferring his place at Yale, he crossed the border into Canada and joined the RCAF on 10th October 1940. At this point in the war, it was technically

John Magee receives his Wings on 16th June 1941 from Group Captain Wilf Curtis

John Magee in a Spitfire

illegal for an American to do this, but the US Government, sympathetic to the allied cause, turned a blind eye.

Flying training progressed well, with him being assessed as an above average, if a little overconfident, pilot. On completion of his training in Canada John boarded the armed British Merchant Ship California, to make the crossing to England. He arrived in July 1941 to undertake his operational training, which included conversion to the Spitfire, on 61 Operational Training Unit at RAF Rednal.

The weather conditions in Canada, which were regularly ideal for flying training meant that part of the conversion course was also to become familiar with Britain's more idiosyncratic weather conditions.

Arriving at RAF Digby in September 1941, he was posted to 412(Falcon) Squadron of the RCAF. Within a month, the squadron moved to the nearby satellite airfield of Wellingore and it is from here that the fateful flight took place.

At 10:40 am, Magee's Spitfire AD291 took off from Wellingore as number three in a flight of four. Whilst by no means dangerous, the weather was uninviting with a low overcast, it was however whilst returning to base, that the weather dealt Magee an unlucky hand.

The flight leader spotted a gap in the cloud and decided to lead his flight down through it in line astern. What nobody knew at the time was that the gap was directly over RAF College Cranwell's circuit. As he followed the other Spitfires down, Magee collided with an Airspeed Oxford which was in the Cranwell circuit.

A farmer later recounted that he saw Magee's spitfire after the collision, the pilot struggled to release the canopy before eventually standing up and jumping from the aircraft. Tragically, Magee was far too low for his parachute to work and he was killed instantly upon hitting the ground.

The Oxford was flown by LAC Ernest Aubrey Griffin, who was undertaking flying training at Cranwell. Whilst flying at 500ft, just below cloud base, Griffin's aircraft was struck from behind by Magee's Spitfire. He too was killed when the aircraft impacted the ground. Both aircraft crashed close to the village of Roxholme, midway between Cranwell and Digby. Griffin, originally from Banbury was laid to rest in nearby Oxford.

Magee's funeral was held two days after the accident on the 13th December. The Squadron provided a bearer party of 45 of his fellow officers,together with representatives from the station's other squadrons (92, 409 and 609) .

On that day in September 1941, when the inspiration for High Flight first struck John Magee, little could he have imagined that his verse would one day travel to the Moon. Just 30 years later, astronaut James Irwin carried the poem with him as captain of Apollo 15, a high flight beyond anyone's dreams in those dark days of war.

High Flight

By John Gillespie Magee

Oh! I have slipped the surly bonds of earth
And danced the skies on laughter-silvered wings;
Sunward I've climbed, and joined the tumbling mirth
Of sun-split clouds, - and done a hundred things
You have not dreamed of - wheeled and soared and swung
High in the sunlit silence. Hov'ring there,
I've chased the shouting wind along, and flung
My eager craft through footless halls of air......

Up,up the long, delirious, burning blue
I've topped the wind-swept heights with easy grace.
Where never lark, or even eagle flew-
And, while with silent, lifting mind I've trod
The high untrespassed sanctity of space,
Put out my hand and touched the face of God.

An Oxford aircraft in war time livery

Sergeant Howard Victor Payne
Royal Canadian Air Force

Died 9th January 1942

In the first few days of 1942 Sergeant Payne was briefed to conduct a Sector Recce from RAF Digby. A sector recce was a routine training exercise for a World War II fighter pilot, testing both their navigational and reconnaissance skills. Having arrived at Digby just a few weeks earlier, during a period of bad weather, this may well have been one of Payne's first flights with 92 Squadron.

His Spitfire BM298 took off at 1400, but did not return. Despite an extensive search of the local area, which continued after dark with the aid of searchlights, nothing was found until two days later. Almost unbelievably, the aircraft had crashed just over a mile from the airfield in Ashby Wood. Despite the delay in finding the wreckage, it was clear that Sergeant Payne had died instantly. However, the cause of the crash was more obscure. The wreckage yielded no clues and since there were no witnesses, it was assumed that he had stalled and spun the aircraft into the ground.

A Digby pilot poses for a photograph with his Spitfire

A testament to the routine nature of these events is the following extract from the Squadron's diary:

'More snow, local flying in the morning. Sgt Payne was buried at Scopwick Cemetery. The Commanding Officer, Flight Commanders and Officers, fellow Sergeant Pilots and other ranks attended the funeral. In the evening a party at the 'Musicians Arms'

Sergeant Payne was described as a rugged outdoor type who had been employed as a Ski Instructor before the war. Originally from Huntsville Ontario, he was just 23 years old at the time of his death.

Flight Sergeant Alexander Ian Murray
Royal Canadian Air Force

Died 19th January 1942

As an aircraft turns, climbs or descends, a person on board will feel the acceleration in the new direction as what is known as G-force. A fairly gentle turn will produce very little G-force, but it is possible for modern fighter pilots to experience as much as 9G. When experiencing 9G, the pilot, and indeed the aircraft will weigh 9 times their normal value. At 2G they would be twice their normal weight, at 3G three times and so on.

In order to maintain level flight, the aircraft must produce an amount of lift which is equal to its weight, if not the aircraft will stall, possibly with serious consequences. If a pilot puts his aircraft into a high G manoeuvre, without taking this into account, it is quite possible for an aircraft that was flying normally to suddenly depart from controlled flight.

Such appears to have been the case whilst Sergeant Murray was at the controls of Beaufighter R2475. The aircraft crashed 5 ½ miles North East of Coleby, the accident report giving the following description of what occurred:

'Sergeant Murray (Pilot) of Beaufighter II R-2475 dived towards ground and commenced to turn to left and pull up at the same time. Aircraft started to roll to left then quickly flicked over to right and hit ground'

Both Murray and his navigator Sergeant Louis Svendsen were killed instantly. Svendsen's body was returned to his family for burial in Portishead, Bristol; whilst Murray was buried with full military honours at Scopwick.

Alexander Murray was born in Schuylerville, New York, to a British father. Before joining up he had worked as a clerk for the Royal Bank of Canada. He had stated in his RCAF application papers that the reason he wished to leave this employment was: *"I'd rather fight the Nazis."*

Flight Lieutenant Jean Henri Marie Offenberg DFC
Royal Air Force

Died 22nd January 1942

Ironically, Jean Offenberg's first action of World War II was against the RAF. As a pilot in the Belgian Air Force, he was sent up in a Fairey Firefly biplane to intercept an RAF Whitley which had inadvertently flown over Belgium whilst returning from a raid on Germany. Belgium was neutral at the time and such measures were seen as essential in maintaining that neutrality.

It had been one minute before midnight on the 8th September 1939 when Whitley K8985 took off from Driffield for a leafleting raid on Germany. On its return in the early hours of the 9th, Jean Offenberg intercepted the aircraft and fired a green flare at it. The Whitley was forced to land at Offenberg's base at Nivelles, where the crew were interned. By the time of the German invasion in May 1940, the crew had already been repatriated, but the Whitley remained on the airfield where it is presumed it was destroyed by advancing German Forces.

During the invasion, Offenberg claimed one Dornier Do17 bomber destroyed and another damaged. But the German Blitz Krieg quickly overtook his country and the squadron had to withdraw to Chatres in France. It quickly became obvious that France too would fall, so Offenberg made his way to Algeria where a Belgian Flying School had been set-up. Joining a group of Poles, he made his way to England via Casablanca and Gibraltar, where he joined the RAF on 30th July 1940.

He converted to the Hurricane at 6 OTU at RAF Sutton Bridge and was operational in time to serve with 145 Squadron during the Battle of Britain. By 1942, he was a highly regarded pilot on 609 (West Riding) Squadron, with five

Flight Lieutenant Offenberg

confirmed victories, another five enemy aircraft probably destroyed and five damaged. On the squadron, he was affectionately known as Pyker and had gained a reputation as a man of great integrity and an inspiration to those around him.

609 Squadron had arrived at Digby in November 1941 and although it was relatively common to see enemy activity in the area, it was a training flight that was to be the cause of Offenberg's death. Offenberg was instructing Pilot Officer Roelandt, a new pilot to the squadron, in formation techniques, and was just about to call it a day, when a Spitfire from 92 Squadron decided to conduct an unplanned mock attack. Despite Offenberg spotting the attack at the last minute, he was unable to avoid the collision.

The 92 Squadron Spitfire took the tail off Offenberg's and both aircraft dived straight into the ground, near Blankney, killing both pilots. The 609 Squadron diary recorded the following:

'This is the saddest day the squadron has endured for many months, for it sees the death of F/L Offenberg, DFC, Croix de Guerre, in an air collision. He was flying in formation with P/O Roelandt when suddenly an aircraft of 92 Sqn (Sgt de Renzl FR), doubtless practicing attack, comes straight for him from above. F/L Offenberg pulls up sharply, but it is too late; the tail unit of his a/c is cut right off, both aircraft hurtle down to the ground, both pilots are killed. So departs one of the kindest and finest leaders.'

Offenberg was buried four days later. Snow lay on the ground as his comrades stood by the graveside. The Countess of Londesborough, who had become a good friend of the squadron, was also present. Dressed in black and carrying a single Lily, she made a striking contrast to the crisp white snow that lay all around them. It is said that when the news of Jean's death was broadcast to Belgium just a few days later, the shock killed his mother. Offenberg's memorial is unique at Scopwick, due to the fact that he is no longer buried there.

After the war his body was repatriated to Belgium and he was reburied in Brussels Town Cemetery. Flying Officer Ziegler was a fellow Belgian pilot on 609 Squadron. His poem about Jean Offenberg provides a moving testament to how highly his comrades regarded him:

Epitaph to a Fighter Pilot

By Flying Officer Ziegler

Here in the corner of an English shire
Far from the homeland he fought to save
A Belgian pilot sleeps, who dying gave,
His all, for all of England to admire.
Here was a warrior of the lonely sky.
Modest and brave, outstanding of his race.
Who winged the outer air with swallow's grace –
To us it hardly seemed that he could die.
And many friends who loved him, and live,
Give thanks to him; his was the magic touch
That plucked them from the death he scorned so much.
And like a shepherd homed them. Do not grieve,
If you should pass this way in after years –
His was a life that shone too bright for tears.

Flight Lieutenant Offenberg's Spitfire - Forestry Commission

Above: The grave marker set in the ground at Scopwick Burial Ground indicating where Flight Lieutenant Offenberg was buried before his body was removed after the war and taken to Belgium
Below: The Belgian Airmen's Field of Honour in Brussels Town Cemetery where Flight Lieutenant Offenberg was reburied in September 1949.

Pilot Officer Robert McConnell Murchie
Royal Canadian Air Force

Died 28th February 1942

Robert Murchie was the pilot of one of two Beaufighters scrambled to meet enemy activity late on the evening of the 28th. At around 23:00hrs, the starboard engine began to fail. What follows is a contemporary account of what happened next, as given to the accident investigation:

'Starboard engine began to vibrate badly at 8,000ft. Pilot was given vector for base and appeared to be handling aircraft satisfactorily, although he steadily lost height. Approximately five minutes after engine failed, pilot told the observer to jump as the engine was on fire. Observer went forward and escaped through the front hatch at about 2,000ft. Aircraft crashed straight into ground and pilot did not escape'

It was thought that once the observer had baled out, Robert tried to do the same. However, as soon as he left the controls the aircraft dived towards the ground, preventing his escape.

Sergeant Andrews, the observer landed near RAF North Coates, while the aircraft crashed just a few miles away at North Thoresby. The next day, the 409 Squadron diary said the following of Robert Murchie: '*In Murchie we lose one of our most reliable men and one of the brightest and most popular officers in our company.*'

Bristol Beaufighter

Robert had been born in Canada, but it appears that he and his family had been living in the USA for some time. He graduated from Marshall High School in Minneapolis, before gaining employment as an apprentice aircraft engineer with Alford Flying Services at Stinson Airport, La Grange, Illinois. When this company was wound-up he moved back to Canada and gained a similar position in Winnipeg.

His aspiration to fly had led him to train towards becoming a pilot at his own expense and by the time he applied to the RCAF, he had amassed fifteen hours of solo flying.

Aircraftman Ireneé Joseph Auguste Gerard St Hilaire
Royal Canadian Air Force

Died 5th March 1942

Aircraftman St Hilaire

Just one day after Robert Murchie's funeral, tragedy was to strike the Canadian community once more. At about 16:00 hrs Aircraftsman St Hilaire was crossing the A 15 near RAF Coleby when he was struck by a passing army lorry. He was taken in an unconscious state to the Station Sick Quarters at Coleby where doctors quickly realised that he had suffered a severe head injury that would require more specialist care.

By 17:30 hrs he had been admitted to the RAF Hospital at Rauceby but, despite the best care that was available at the time, St Hilaire's condition continued to deteriorate and by 19:30hrs he had died.

Ireneé St Hilaire was a French Canadian from Montreal. Before the war he had served an apprenticeship as a welder. He had originally joined the Canadian Army but transferred to the RCAF in May 1941, where he became an aero engine mechanic.

It is interesting to note that the spelling of Ireneé is at variance with what is on the gravestone, but service records confirm that Ireneé is in fact correct. The authors have notified the Commonwealth War Graves Commission and hopefully, in time, this error will be rectified.

Squadron Leader Bruce Alexander Hanbury
Royal Canadian Air Force

Pilot Officer Philip Marcus Sweet
Royal Canadian Air Force

Flight Sergeant John William Dickson
Royal Canadian Air Force

Died 27th March 1942

Sqn Ldr Hanbury

The twin engine Bristol Beaufighter became an extremely capable night-fighter, but as so often the case with advanced aircraft, it had its vices. Should the aircraft be stalled, it had the tendency to flick violently onto its back and enter a spin. To compound the problem, the severity of the manoeuvre could also cause the engine to stall and if the stalled engine happened to be the one on the inside of the spin, recovery was almost impossible.

409 Squadron were fully aware of these issues and to minimise the risk, they had adopted a policy of taking new pilots on a familiarisation flight where they could experience both the Beaufighter's stall characteristics and recovery procedures with an experienced pilot. So it was that, just two days after arriving on the squadron, Pilot Officer Sweet was taken up by Sqn Ldr Hanbury for a stall demonstration in Beaufighter T3142. As the aircraft flew over East Leake near Boston, numerous eye witnesses saw what happened before the aircraft finally crashed at Lexeton Dutgate.

Mr Austin Monks, a private pilot before the war, gave the following statement:

"It did a right hand roll and recovered perfectly and then flew level for about half a mile and did another. It did not appear to lose height on the first roll. He came out of the second roll very slowly and with the nose very high. Both rolls were right-handed. As he came out of the second roll, he suddenly flicked over into a right hand spin. It looked to me as though he had the stick a little too far back as he came out of the second roll. It was quite a flat spin and he came down slowly. One engine cut on the second roll. There was a burst of engine after one or two flicks of the spin. The spin was very vicious at first. As it came down I could see that the starboard engine was cut. At about 4,000 feet

the pilot appeared to get the aeroplane under control and I thought that he was going to over correct, the nose was fairly high in the correction. It flicked back into a spin again and spun down into the ground. The pilot was obviously wrestling with the machine all the time."

Other witness including Mr C F Dunn, a Royal Observer Corps Post Commander, broadly agreed with this version:

"At 15:30hrs on 27th March 1942 I was on duty at G1 post ,Old Leake. When I first saw it, it was flying south east and straight and level when suddenly it appeared to do a victory roll. It continued rolling with the fuselage horizontal. At about 8,000 feet it started to spin. It was spinning clockwise"

These and other witnesses seem to confirm that the aircraft was in a right-hand spin with the right-hand engine stopped, a fatal combination. The description of victory rolls by many of the witnesses caused some consternation for the commanding officer of 409 Squadron, as no such aerobatics had been authorised as part of this sortie.

The Commanding Officer had the following to say on the matter:

"I knew Squadron Leader Hanbury very well personally and I am sure that he would never carry out intentional aerobatics in a Beaufighter. Therefore I am inclined to doubt the accuracy of the witnesses as the manoeuvres which they described as victory rolls"

A plausible explanation of events is that Squadron Leader Hanbury was demonstrating a stall in the approach configuration. Crash investigators and witnesses both confirmed that the flaps and undercarriage were down at the time. In this configuration, it was known that the aircraft could flick violently onto its back as it stalled, this may have appeared as a victory roll to those on the ground. It was also possible that the violence of this flick, could also have caused the starboard engine to cut, making recovery very difficult.

Squadron Leader Hanbury was from Vancouver, British Columbia and completed a degree at McGill University. He then worked as an aircraft dispatcher for Trans Canadian Airlines, whilst joining the 72nd Seaforth Highlanders as an armourer in 1934. Two years later, he transferred to the Royal Canadian Air Force. At first he served in a ground role, but by early 1940 he had qualified as a pilot.

Pilot Officer Sweet's original grave marker

On 23rd December 1939, he married his wife Nancy Hope Hanbury, shipping out to England just a short time later. Arriving in England at the height of the Battle of Britain, he first flew the Lysander with 112 Squadron. Volunteering for a transfer to Fighter Command he was posted to RAF Wittering to fly Hurricanes with 1 Sqn.

Pilot Officer Sweet was an American citizen from Huron, South Dakota where he had worked as an acrobat in a circus. He had joined the RCAF in October 1940 as a pilot. Having completed his training, he was posted to 60 Operational Training Unit at East Fortune in Scotland. It was here that he was to have an unfortunate accident whilst landing a Blenheim.

The report makes it clear that the hierarchy were not impressed, but the result of a quicker posting to an operational fighter squadron is unlikely to have caused Sweet too much worry:

'Pilot Officer Sweet is a staff pilot at this unit – not an instructor. He is a keen pilot and has been very useful. Even if hydraulics were sluggish this accident savours a very slack flying which is doubly serious since the flight was a demonstration to a pupil. Although an extremely keen American pilot, Pilot Officer Sweet is not suitable as an instructor and his posting to an operational unit has been recommended'

Sergeant Dickson was the Air Gunner on board that night. He was originally from Toronto, having joined the RCAF at the very outbreak of war. Just seven months before his death, he had survived a crash landing in a Defiant which had left him hospitalised.

Flight Sergeant George Stanley Gould
Royal Canadian Air Force

Died 10th April 1942

1426 (Enemy Aircraft) Flight had been formed in November 1941, their task being to test and evaluate captured enemy aircraft. Further to that, they also toured RAF stations to give operational crews a close look at the aircraft they would be flying against.

Although their aircraft were painted in RAF colours, it was thought that an aircraft positively identified as a German type would still be attacked, the pilot perhaps suspecting subterfuge. For this reason, whenever 1426 Flt's aircraft were transiting around the country, they always received an RAF fighter escort.

Such was the case on 10th April 1942, when 412 Squadron were tasked with escorting some of 1426 Flt's German aircraft back to their base, following a visit to RAF Waddington. Just one mile south of Waddington, two Spitfires which had been weaving amongst the formation of German aircraft, collided.

Gould's Spitfire (AD305) was struck by another flown by Flight Lieutenant Napier. Gould lost the tail to his aircraft and died in the ensuing crash. Napier was more fortunate and was able to make a crash landing. However, he suffered serious injuries in the crash, including a fractured skull.

The reason for the collision is not known, but it is possible that both pilots became distracted by being so close to enemy aircraft, that they didn't pay the correct attention to the lookout for each other.

A Messerschmitt 109 in RAF colours belonging to 1426 (Enemy Aircraft) Flight

George Harrod
2nd Kesteven Battalion, Home Guard

Died 24th June 1942

George as a young man

George Harrod was not on military duty when his accident befell him, he was in fact on a routine errand for his employers, G W Parker's. A large estate at the time, Parker's later became the Blankney Estates. Employed as a Wagoner, George was collecting a recently repaired wagon from the wheelwrights in Metheringham and once a weighing machine had been loaded, he set off on his way.

Almost immediately, the horse pulling the wagon bolted and began galloping as fast as it could. At the junction of Metheringham High Street and Station Road the near-side of the wagon struck a wall and George was thrown from the wagon. Witnesses recalled seeing a grey car overtake the horse and wagon, but they were quite insistent that there was nothing unusual in the way it was being driven and certainly should not have spooked the horse. George was mortally injured. Tragically, two of

2nd Kesteven Battalion of the Home Guard

George's four children stumbled upon the accident scene on their way to school, but a local woman thoughtfully shielded them from the site and told them to go to school.

The funeral was held the following Sunday and was attended by members of the Home Guard and representatives from his employer. In a heart-warming gesture, the company stood by their former employee and provided a house for his widow and four children, the youngest of which was only six weeks old at the time of his death.

His daughter Rosemarie, who was just three years old at the time of the accident, recalls the post-war dedication of the cross of sacrifice at Scopwick:

"I remember going as a child to the dedication of the big cross and headstones at Scopwick Church and graveyard. We all marched from the church to the graveyard in a procession, the vicar and RAF superiors in the front"

Flying Officer William Derry Gibson
Royal Canadian Air Force

Died 19th September 1942

Flying Officer Gibson had taken off from RAF Coleby Grange on an operational night-fighter patrol in Beaufighter X8106. Not long into that patrol he radioed base to inform them that he had only 10 pounds of oil pressure in his starboard engine and that he was returning to base.

On return to base at 21:55 hrs, the starboard engine had either failed completely or been shut down by Gibson as a precautionary measure. His initial approach was good, but he became a little high, touching down 700 yards beyond the threshold of the runway and bouncing the aircraft back into the air. By now the aircraft was well to the left of the runway centre line and in the dark it is highly probable that he could not see the brick buildings in front of him.

The aircraft struck the station post office, demolishing it completely. Gibson was killed instantaneously, but his observer's life was to be saved by some remarkable courage which was to be rewarded with a British Empire Medal. The citation for LAC Howard Carter's medal reads as follows:

'One night in September 1942, an aircraft struck a stores hut on an airfield and burst into flames. LAC Carter and another airman who were working nearby hastened to the scene of the crash and on arrival found that the perspex of the observer's astrodome was broken. Despite the fact that the front of the aircraft was burning fiercely and the remaining petrol tanks were likely to explode, LAC Carter climbed through the hole in the perspex in an endeavour to rescue the observer, who was in the middle of the aircraft and lying across the ammunition tank. He had some difficulty in raising the observer as a cord of the latter's helmet was wound around his face and caught by a projection in the aircraft, but Carter succeeded in freeing his comrade and in getting him under the astrodome. The other airman had, in the meantime, broken away pieces of the perspex and with his assistance Carter lifted the observer out of the aircraft just as the ammunition began to explode. His courageous action undoubtedly saved the observer's life.'

LAC Carter had originally been recommended for the award of the George Medal. LAC Corbeill, who assisted him received a Mention in Dispatches despite being recommended for the British Empire Medal. The rescued Observer Sergeant B A Leehy, suffered serious injuries, but is thought to have recovered in hospital.

Before the war, William Gibson was a Bank Clerk for the Imperial Bank of Canada in Saskatoon. He had joined the RCAF in November 1940 and was awarded his pilot's wings in August 1941. He had been with 409 Squadron since February 1942.

RCAF Intelligence Officer at work.

Four young Sergeant pilots enjoying a moments relaxation

Flying Officer Kenneth Earle Warner
Royal Canadian Air Force

Sergeant Herbert Pendleton
Royal Air Force

Died 5th December 1942

Kenneth Earle Warner

Flying Officer Warner and Sergeant Pendleton had joined 409 Squadron only 10 days previously, it was a clear starry night and they were tasked with a Ground Controlled Intercept training flight.

At around 22:30 Kenneth Warner, the Beaufighter's pilot, began to experience problems. He was at 8,000 feet and reported that his starboard engine had begun to run rough.

He began a slow descent, but as he did so the engine caught fire. By this time he was at 800 feet and reported that the glare from the engine fire had blinded him to such an extent, that he was unable to see his instruments. He was advised to climb a little higher and abandon the aircraft, but at 22:40 hours, Beaufighter X8140 crashed at Langwith Colliery north of Mansfield. Both occupants were killed by the impact.

Kenneth Warner was an American citizen from Lexington, Oregon. He had spent 4 years in the US Navy aboard the American battleship, USS Idaho. Leaving the Navy in 1940, he had returned home, where he worked as a farm labourer. However, after only one year he left home to join the RCAF.

Sergeant Pendleton was an RAF Observer who was married and was from East Croydon.

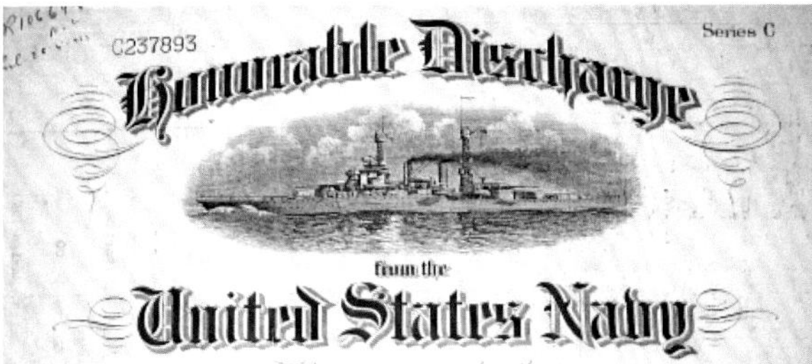

C237893 Series C

Honourable Discharge

from the

United States Navy

This is to certify that
Kenneth Earle Warner a Storekeeper Third Class
is Honourably Discharged from the United States Ship
Idaho and from the Naval Service of the United States
this 12th day of January, 1940.
This certificate is awarded as a Testimonial of Fidelity and Obedience.

Charles E Olsen
Lieut. Commander, U.S.N.

Kenneth Warner's Honourable Discharge Certificate from USS Idaho

Pilot Officer Hunter George Wilberforce Smith
Royal Australian Air Force

Died 10th December 1942

At 14:25 hours Hunter Smith took off from RAF Digby in a 288 Squadron Hurricane W9244, his mission was routine anti-aircraft cooperation training over Scunthorpe. Such a mission would usually involve acting as an airborne target for anti-aircraft gunners to train their guns on, though no rounds would actually be fired.

Just 25 minutes after take-off he radioed to say that his aircraft was on fire. He was seen to circle with his undercarriage up and smoke coming from the engine. Whilst attempting to make a forced landing, at Ashby near Scunthorpe, his aircraft dived in from 50 feet, killing him instantly. The subsequent investigation found that the Merlin engine's big-end had failed, puncturing an eight inch hole in the side of the crankcase. The catastrophic damage to the engine not only resulted in a total loss of power, but also caused a major fire in the aircraft.

Hunter was an Australian from Woollahra, New South Wales. He was an experienced pilot with just under 800 hours of flying under his belt. At the time of the accident he was a Sergeant; however, unbeknown to him, he had been commissioned as a Pilot Officer. Sadly news of this only came through after his death.

Flight Sergeant James Douglas Barbour
Royal Canadian Air Force

Died 13th December 1942

Flight Sergeant Barbour

Flight Sergeant Barbour was a Spitfire pilot belonging to 411 Squadron RCAF. On the 13th December, he was conducting bomber affiliation with Lancasters, vital training during which the bomber's pilot and gunners could practice fending off a fighter attack.

It was thought at the time that, whilst at low level, he got into the bomber's slipstream and lost control of the aircraft. Spitfire AB283 crashed at Thornton-Le-Fen near Boston, killing James instantly.

Before joining the RCAF, James had been a clerk for the Canada Bread Company in Toronto. His hobbies included hockey, basketball, swimming and skiing. At the time of his death, he had been on 411 Squadron for less than four months.

Leading Aircraftman Charles Fortune Hutton
Royal Canadian Air Force

Died 19th December 1942

LAC Hutton

Charles Hutton was educated at Upper Canada College, Toronto and entered the service of the Canadian Bank of Commerce 28th September, 1933. He served at Toronto city branches, Newcastle and Oshawa before enlisting into the RCAF on 28th August, 1941. During his initial RCAF medical it was discovered that he had defective colour vision, with the medical officer remarking that it was unsafe. Whether or not he had ambitions to become aircrew, this undoubtedly put an end to it.

Undeterred, he joined as an administrative clerk and worked within the Accounts Flight at Digby. His previous experience as a bank clerk must have made him an obvious choice for this position. Charles had arrived at Digby in the April of 1942 and had become a popular member of the section.

On the 30th November, Charles went to the Station sick Quarters complaining of feeling unwell. Here they diagnosed a case of acute Bronchitis and admitted him immediately. Over the next few days his condition worsened and he was transferred to the RAF Hospital at Rauceby, but on the 19th of December he died. A post mortem later determined the cause of death as a cerebral thrombosis.

The Senior Accounts Officer wrote to Charles' mother describing the memorial service held for him:

'Arrangements were made with the vicar of the church in the little village in which the accounts office is situated, to hold a memorial service on Sunday the 20th. I can assure you that this was a very impressive spectacle. All members of the accounts section attended, and special hymns, chosen by the staff, were sung. A silk RCAF ensign was placed over the alter, and the clergyman preached a very beautiful sermon, saying among other things how much he would miss Charles, who had attended this church, from time to time.'

Time to relax with a game of cards

Warrant Officer II Bernard Higson Barber
Royal Canadian Air Force

Flying Officer William Bertram Mosley
Royal Canadian Air Force

Flying Officer Harry Brooks
Royal Canadian Air Force

Warrant Officer I Henry Hare
Royal Canadian Air Force

Died 31st December 1942

Bullseye exercises allowed bomber crews to practice attacks against British cities, honing their skills before employing them on operational missions against Germany. The exercises were made as realistic as possible, with the bombers facing searchlight defences and night-fighter attack.

For the pilots of the night-fighters, the exercises did offer valuable training, but patrolling the same piece of darkened sky for hours on end could get tedious. On New Year's Eve 1942, two Beaufighters of 409 Squadron, call signs Ragbag 18 and Ragbag 25, took off from Coleby Grange. The Fighter Controller in the Digby Sector Operations Room vectored them northwest and handed them over to his colleague at Kirton in Lindsey.

The Kirton controller allocated each aircraft a fighter box, these were pieces of airspace of defined dimension each with a radio beacon. The controller would have expected each pilot to orbit their respective beacons until he gave them instructions to do otherwise.

However, it would appear that the pilots of both aircraft had different ideas. Ragbag 25 was initially well to the east of his beacon and whilst being ordered back, he carried out an unauthorised intercept of a Wellington bomber. In the subsequent enquiry, the controller gave the following evidence:

"I then rang the Digby Controller to query whether he, Ragbag 25, knew the drill at all and he said he was quite OK and had bags of experience........Major Scott and myself were getting rather peeved at his wanderings and Major Scott said something to the effect that it was no good trying to do an exercise if the pilots did not stick to the rules."

At length, the controller was able to persuade Ragbag 25 to maintain on his beacon and from the controller's perspective the intercepts started to go much better. Meanwhile Ragbag 18 flown by the less experienced Sergeant Barber was having difficulty locating his beacon. After receiving 15 fixes, he did eventually locate it, but he too had a tendency to wander off chasing contacts shown on his own radar set.

Just three minutes before the accident Ragbag 25 reported searchlights, possibly indicating the presence of a target aircraft. The controller vectored him towards these. At the same time Ragbag 18 was chasing his own radar contact and strayed into Ragbag 25's area whilst doing so.

At 1853 hrs, Barber's aircraft sliced into the back of Ragbag 25 taking off the entire tail unit together with a large part of the starboard wing. Whether Sergeant Barber was chasing the same target as Ragbag 25 or indeed Ragbag 25 itself will never be known.

Sergeant Barber's aircraft crashed on Noel Street in Gainsborough, demolishing three houses and damaging 20 others. Sadly, as well as both of the crew, a three year old girl was killed. Dave French, a relative takes up the story:

A copy of the original picture of Margaret Ann recovered from the rubble of the house

"Mother lived at No. 2 Noel Street with her parents Charles and Mary Jane Tedds and her sister Lily. Her two brothers were in the army and not at home. Her elder sister Ivy had married Guy Eames and they lived next door at No. 4 Noel Street. Mother had got back from her shift at a local factory and remembers it was about 7 o'clock when the plane came down, crashing directly in front of No. 4 and damaging and setting fire to No's 2, 4, and 6. Sister Lily was burnt but recovered, Ivy's young daughter Margaret Ann was trapped in No 4 and died of burns. One of the few things mother recovered from the rubble was a part burnt photo of the little girl. It seems a six year old girl from no. 8 Noel Street was in no. 6 just before the crash. She wanted to go home to put some money in her piggy bank, little Margaret wanted to go with her but was told to stay, so was in the house when it was hit. Pure bad luck."

With burning aviation fuel and exploding ammunition, Noel Street was a scene of total devastation, the local Newspaper told of one tale of heroism amongst the carnage:

'Three daughters of Mr & Mrs C W Tedds were having tea when the plane crashed. Mrs Tedds was ill in bed upstairs. Her daughters escaped by the back door, but Mrs Tedds was trapped. A neighbour, Mr G Bingham, ran into the blazing house and carried her to safety. Mr S Brooks who lives near said "It was a gallant rescue, Bingham risked his life as the place was an inferno and bullets were going off in all directions.'

Ragbag 25 came down in open land close to the general cemetery near Corringham. Due to the fact that the aircraft had not exploded on impact, it was not found until the next day. Both airmen on board were dead. The crews of each aircraft were as follows:

Beaufighter VI X8192 - Ragbag 25, crashed Corringham.
Pilot Officer H Brooks - Pilot
Pilot Officer W B Mosley - Observer.

Beaufighter VI EL184 - Ragbag 18, crashed Noel Street Gainsborough.
Sergeant B H Barber - Pilot
Flight Sergeant H Hare - Observer.

In an ironic turn of events, news of each of their promotions came through just after their deaths.

Bernard Barber

Harry Brooks was from Quebec in Canada, where he had worked as an airline despatcher for Canadian Colonial Airways Limited. He was an extremely keen sportsman and had joined the RCAF in August 1940. Although he himself was a native Canadian, his mother was born in Leeds and his father in Lincoln. William Mosley was from London, Ontario. Just two months before the accident, he had married Susannah Fox in Coleby Church. In the years prior to joining the RCAF, he had undertaken part-time office work. Bernard Barber was originally from Vernon, British Columbia, his interviewer at his initial RCAF interview said of him: *'Quiet determined type. Neatly dressed and of good appearance. Should be good pilot material'*

Before the war, Henry Hare was employed as a Lab Assistant at the Imperial Varnish and Colour Company in Toronto. He listed his hobbies as building model boats and aeroplanes.

Obergerfreiter Karl Heinz Krusewitz
German Luftwaffe

Unteroffizier Kurt Semlitschka
German Luftwaffe

Unteroffizier Helmut Knorr
German Luftwaffe

Leutnant Gunther Wolff
German Luftwaffe

Died 15th January 1943

On the night of 15th January 1945, Lincoln came under attack from the Luftwaffe, six high explosive bombs and 111 incendiary devices fell across the city, but Avondale and Thomas Street were particularly badly hit. A NAAFI girl was killed when the bus she was travelling in was hit by an incendiary bomb and an airman from Digby, who happened to be in Lincoln, lost an arm. There were several other fatalities across the city as well as a chemist shop, warehouses and a bank being substantially damaged.

The cause of all this havoc was a Dornier Do 217 of 7/KG2, but its success was to be short lived. A Mosquito of 151 Squadron based at RAF Wittering was about to intercept the enemy raider, their combat report tells what happened next:

INTELLIGENCE REPORT "N"
(Defensive Night Patrol)
From:- RAF Wittering (Intelligence)
To:- No. 12 Group (Intelligence)

GENERAL REPORT

Sergeant E A Knight (Canadian) Firework 53 with Sergeant V I L Roberts left Wittering at 20:25 hours and returned at 21:45 hours. They were taken over by Patrington Ground Controlled Intercept Station at 20:40 hours to intercept enemy aircraft coming in from the East Coast and after vectors of 360° and 290° a contact was obtained at maximum range (height 10,500ft) at 20:42 hours. Enemy aircraft was reported going 290° at 180 mph, but this is considered underestimated as Mosquito at 220-230 mph failed to catch up until speed was increased.

Owing to interference this contact was lost and Sergeant Roberts switched off the Pilot Indicator and saw the blip disappear into the ground return. Control was then asked for help, and a few minutes later contact was regained on a jinking target at maximum range and Mosquito closed rapidly to 5000ft when reflected signal was too strong for interference to be effective.

At 3,500ft range a visual of a Dornier 217 was obtained, height still about 10,500ft, but at this point enemy aircraft dived to port down to 4,000ft and its evasive action consisted of left and right hand turns and complete circuits. Sergeant Knight's first burst was fired from ¼ astern just as enemy aircraft began its first dive and the port engine was hit.

Return fire (machine gun from dorsal position) was experienced passing over starboard wing tip, but after Knight's second burst from starboard side, which hit the starboard engine, this return fire ceased. A third burst on the fuselage from port quarter astern caused pieces of the aircraft to fly off, and with both engines blazing, enemy aircraft dived steeply from 4,000ft into a field where it exploded.

The range had been 150 yards and less and the Mosquito suffered superficial damage through pieces of the enemy aircraft hitting it. Cannon only was used (311 rounds). This was Sgt Knight's first operational sortie. Controllers name:- Squadron Leader Donaldson. This DO 217 is claimed as destroyed.

Pilot and Navigator of a Mosquito with ground crew.

Two pictures of the damage to Lincoln caused by the bombing

The aircraft had come down in a field near Boothby Graffoe, just south of Lincoln killing the four German crew members. This location fell within the jurisdiction of RAF Digby, who organised a military funeral with due honours at Scopwick.

At the end of the war, the vast majority of Germans who had been buried in local churchyards around the country were re-interred at Cannock Chase in the West Midlands. The few exceptions to this occurred when the local populace and the German families were happy for them to remain in their original graves. It is assumed that such was the case in this instance.

Sergeant Knight claimed a second kill in February 1944 when he shot down a Messerschmitt Bf 110. However, he and his navigator were killed just four days later when he crashed his Mosquito into the channel.

Warrant Officer II John Alexander McMillan
Royal Canadian Air Force

Died 21st January 1943

Warrant Officer McMillan had made an inauspicious start to his life on 411 Squadron. Just weeks after joining them, he forget to put the undercarriage of his Spitfire down before landing. The fact that it was night time and he was a very inexperienced pilot cut little ice with his Commanding Officer and he was sent on an aircrew refresher course at Brighton, from which he returned on 27th November 1942.

On the 21st January, McMillan was airborne with his squadron on a gunnery practice. On completion of the exercise, they were returning to base and approaching the coastline near Skegness, when McMillan's Spitfire AA754 was in collision with a Cranwell based Lysander V9797. Both aircraft crashed into the Sea and despite a search by an Air Sea Rescue launch, no trace of McMillan was found. His body washed up on the shore at Chapel St Leonard some days later.

John McMillan was originally from Winnipeg, Manitoba, where he was born, educated and worked as a packer.

An RCAF Spitfire pilot dressed for cold weather and ready for action

Pilot Officer Gilbert Frederick Brown
Royal Canadian Air Force

Died 28th January 1943

Gilbert Brown on enlisting

Fighter pilots spent many hours training in World War II, an inexperienced pilot was easy prey for the Luftwaffe. In order to assess how effective each pilot had been during these mock dog-fights, a cine camera took the role of the aircraft's guns. When the pilot pressed the trigger, the camera began to film where the guns were aiming and in this way it could later be judged whether or not he had managed to shoot the aircraft down. On the 28th January, two 411 Squadron Spitfires were engaged in a cine-gun exercise over Orby near Skegness. At 11:35 disaster struck and the two aircraft collided. Pilot Officer Graham, the surviving pilot was later able to give the following account:

"At 11:25 hours 28th January 1943, Pilot Officer Brown and myself were orbiting Skegness at roughly 11,000ft, on a tail-chase exercise, to be followed by a Cine Gun exercise. Pilot Officer Brown called up "You keep on my tail" (I was about 200 yards behind him at the time). He then proceeded to try and lose me, using orthodox manoeuvres. Then he did a complete roll on top of a loop – I followed with a half roll. This brought me behind and beneath him with a difference of about 100 feet between us. Pilot Officer Brown's aircraft then seemed to stall on top of me – I saw this coming, tried to turn to starboard, but was so close to stalling that the controls did not react quickly enough. The aircraft collided – I ducked my head and crouched down in the cockpit. When I sat up again my aircraft was spinning and bucking hard. I tried to pull out of the spin, but the controls were loose and dead. I then opened the hood; (lost my helmet) undid the safety straps, and pushed myself out. I remember a tear at my right leg as I left the aircraft. (The height was now about 7,000ft) This was caused by the aerial mast, I believe. The aircraft seemed to slide away from me, and I pulled the rip-cord of my parachute. I remember seeing my aircraft spinning down without a tail unit, and looking up above me and seeing a tail unit floating down – I did not see Pilot Officer Brown's aircraft again at all."

It was later determined that Brown's aircraft had taken off the tail of Graham's with its port wing. The port wing of Brown's aircraft had also been sheared off just outboard of the guns. Brown's Spitfire, AB847 crashed in Orby

Marshes about one mile east of Orby village. Graham's Spitfire, R6879 crashed about one mile south of this.

Gilbert Brown was a married man and had a five month-old son back in Canada. He had worked as a Stock Controller for an engineering firm in Toronto.

Warrant Officer II Benjamin Merwin Haight
Royal Canadian Air Force

Sergeant Oswald Sidwell Milburn BA
Royal Air Force

Died 19th March 1943

On 22nd January 1943, Sergeant Haight had secured 410 Squadron's first kill when he engaged a Dornier Do 217 off the northeast coast. His first salvo set one of the Dornier's engines alight and after the second the aircraft spiralled steeply down into cloud. Although lost from Haight's sight, the Royal Observer Corps were able to confirm the enemy aircraft had crashed into the sea five miles off Hartlepool.

Haight and Milburn had a close shave a few nights later, whilst returning to their base at Acklington. Their Mosquito's windscreen had iced over causing Haight, the pilot, to overshoot his landing. The aircraft narrowly missed the control tower and hit a small building. Despite the aircraft being destroyed, the only injuries were cuts and bruises to the occupant of the building.

On 19th March, their luck finally ran out, returning from an operational patrol, their Mosquito HJ930 crashed one mile northeast of Coleby Grange whilst attempting to land. Both were killed. It was thought possible that they might have been dazzled by searchlights.

Their funerals were held at Scopwick three days later and unusually for wartime, both Haight's parents were in attendance. Benjamin Haight was from Sudbury, Ontario, he had been born there to American parents

Oswald Milburn was from Grange-over-Sands in Cumbria and had received a Bachelor of Arts degree from Oxford University.

Flying Officer Norman Alexander Watt
Royal Canadian Air Force

Died 1st July 1943

Norman Watt

Flying Officer Norman Watt was flying a tail-chase exercise with two other Spitfire pilots, Pilot Officer Phillip and Sergeant Chalot. At approximately 10:30, Watt's Spitfire entered a spin from 6,000ft and crashed into a field three miles east of Dorrington near Sleaford. The aircraft buried itself deeply in the marshy land, and remained there for the next 46 years.

In 1989 a group of aviation enthusiast conducted an excavation to recover the remains of the Spitfire. The pieces of recovered airframe were reconstructed and now form an extremely poignant display at the Lincolnshire Aviation Heritage Centre at East Kirkby. The excavation also produced an unexpected find, still lying within the cockpit were Norman's remains.

Given that a burial had occurred in 1943, the excavation team were quite shocked to find this. Positive identification was achieved when they found Norman's well preserved wallet, which included a leave application for 29th June to 2nd July

Norman Watt's Spitfire remains on show at East Kirkby

As was quite often the case in the war, the Air Force had neither the means nor the time to recover a pilot's body which was deeply buried in marshy ground, so they just buried what they could find.

On 10th October 1989 the RAF gathered around Norman's grave for a second time, this time with his two sisters and other relatives from Canada present. It had taken nearly 50 years, but Norman was finally laid to rest in Scopwick. Norman was from Merrickville, Ontario where he had worked as a Tinter in the Ottawa Paint Works.

Spitfire BL655 had been donated by the British community in Argentina under the auspices of the Wings for Winston Foundation of Buenos Aires and had been named Hurlingham.

Norman came from a military family, his father, still a serving soldier had served in the First World War during which he had lost two brothers. Two of Norman's brothers also fought in the Second World War; Alistair was a Lancaster Bomber pilot who was killed on his twentieth operational mission, a raid on Nuremburg in March 1945.

His second brother Cecil was badly injured in Falaise in north west France in August 1944, not long after the D-Day invasion. Such was the extent of his injuries, he had to be permanently evacuated back to Canada.

It should be noted that a number of sources state that Norman was shot down in combat, this was categorically not the case, as documentary evidence proves it was a training accident.

Spitfire BL655 having arrived on the squadron

Warrant Officer II William Balduff
Royal Canadian Air Force

Died 29th July 1943

William Balduff

When America entered the war in December 1941, following the Japanese attack on Pearl Harbour, those of its citizens who had already joined the RAF and RCAF were offered the opportunity to transfer to the United States Army Air Force. However, a substantial number, including William Balduff of Tulsa, elected to stay.

In August 1941 William had travelled to Toronto to join the RCAF, where he was found suitable for training as a pilot. He gained his wings in July 1942 and arrived in England on 19th August. His first operational unit was 277 Squadron, but by August 1943 he had joined 416 Squadron.

It can only be surmised why William decided to visit Polebrook in the squadron's Tiger Moth, but it is reasonable to assume that, since the former RAF airfield had been handed over to the American Eighth Air Force just a month earlier, he may have been visiting some American friends.

The Tiger Moth is a relatively benign biplane trainer, especially when compared to the cutting edge fighters he was used to flying. However, they can easily prove lethal. The cause of the demise of Tiger Moth EK805 and its pilot is not known, but the crash at Polebrook airfield killed William instantly. The Squadron diary said of him:

'Sergeant Balduff was a typical yank in the RCAF, who did not want to transfer to the USAAF and was liked by the pilots and ground crew very much.'

A Tiger Moth similar to that flown by William Balduff

Essential services on station. Above - Station workshops.
Below - The Operations Centre

Flying Officer Peter Ronald Benjamin Littlewood
Royal Air Force

Flight Lieutenant Elbert Alonzo Murray
Royal Canadian Air Force

Died 30th July 1943

410 Squadron's operational aircraft was the Mosquito, but they also had the use of an Airspeed Oxford for training and communications purposes. On the day in question, Flight Lieutenant Murray was acting as a Flight Commander whilst the usual incumbent, Squadron Leader A G Lawrence, was on leave. Having checked the meteorological report and correctly authorised the flight in the Oxford, Murray together with his navigator Flying Officer Littlewood, set off on a navigation training exercise to RAF Colerne.

The next time Murray's Oxford was spotted, it was 15 miles off course over RAF Honiley in Warwickshire. Just after 1600 hours events took a dramatic turn for the worse, Flight Sergeant Craven later recalled what he saw:

"I am a pilot of 285 squadron stationed at RAF Honiley. I was proceeding from the 285 Squadron hangar to the flight dispersal when I noticed an Oxford aircraft about 3 miles to the west at about 2,500ft. Thinking that it was one of our own aircraft I waited to watch it make an approach. I saw the nose of the aircraft drop slightly and then regain its normal attitude, then the nose dropped again rather violently and the machine went into a dive and disappeared behind some trees just southwest of the aerodrome. I could not hear the engines of the aircraft because of another aircraft taxying near me. I did not see the aircraft reappear so I informed the Flying Control Officer by telephone"

There were many other witnesses to the accident and all their accounts were pretty consistent. The aircraft was flying along quite normally at about 2-3000 feet, when it suddenly entered a near vertical dive and crashed into Hay's Wood, near Honiley. The accident investigation team had little to go on, the wreckage showed there was no mechanical reason why the aircraft should have crashed and the pilot was known to be very capable and experienced.

The investigation did highlight a number of interesting pieces of evidence. It was an extremely hot day, the aircraft was 15 miles off course and both aircrew had taken their flying helmets off. Due to this it was hypothesised that they may have been suffering from heat stroke. By no means conclusive, the definitive cause of this crash will probably remain a mystery.

Murray and Littlewood were both Canadians, but it appears that rather than adopting the usual route of joining the RCAF, Littlewood travelled to England and joined the RAF directly. Elbert Murray was from Stellarton, Nova Scotia and Peter Littlewood was from Saanichton, Vancouver Island.

One possible explanation for Peter's unusual route into the RAF was that his brother, Maurice had done the same in 1940. Maurice was a Whitley bomber pilot flying from Dishforth. He was shot down and killed over Kiel, at the age of 22, the same age Peter was when he died two years later.

In January 1944, both men were awarded a posthumous Mention in Dispatches following their shared claim of a BV138 flying boat on the 19th June 1934 and their own Dornier Do 217 on 25/26th July 1943.

Flying Officer Harry James Kirton
Royal Canadian Air Force

Died 13th January 1944

The imminent arrival of a weather front prompted the commanding officer of 409 Squadron to cancel all training flights from Coleby Grange that evening. However it was not all bad news for the squadron as bases in southern England were much worse off and 409 Squadron were drafted in to bolster the defences:

'The whole flight was called to immediate readiness and high spirits resulted at the prospect of joy at Jerry's expense.'

Later that night, two Beaufighters were scrambled against German intruders, the crews had to contend with thick cloud, rain and ice. Whilst it was not totally unflyable, a pilot would certainly need to have his wits about him and any unserviceability in the aircraft could have dramatic consequences.

Flying Officer George West, was later able to give this account of what befell his aircraft:

"On January 13/44 we were scrambled from Coleby Grange Air Field with instructions to make 12,000ft on a course of 170 which was later changed

to 155. It was raining and we entered cloud at 1,100 feet and as far as I was able to judge we climbed through cloud to the given height and were still in it. After flying at this height for approximately five minutes the artificial horizon indicated the aircraft was flying slightly port wing high. I corrected for this and found it necessary to make another correction to lower the port wing. My airspeed at first was indicating 180 mph. Upon correcting for the artificial horizon it dropped to 170 mph. The rate of climb and descent then rose from the neutral position to indicate a climb of 500ft per minute but immediately descended to indicate a drop of 2,500ft per minute. The directional gyro then indicated a turn to port.

The artificial horizon was now showing that the aircraft was in straight and level flight. I tried the other suction valve, but the horizon and direction gyro remained the same. Then by opening the throttle I tried to correct the turn but with no effect. I checked to see if the pitot heat switch was on and it was. I could see no visual horizon. While operating the port throttle I gave the Navigator instructions to abandon the aircraft; he acknowledged me. After 10 seconds I asked him if he had jumped he replied, "No – not yet". I told him, "Hurry up - jump" and in the meantime prepared to jump myself. I collapsed the seat and cut switches and said to him "Jumping." While climbing out one of my feet knocked the switches to the on position.

The escape hatch opened immediately and before dropping myself out I looked back to his seat, but was only able to see the back of it. The height I abandoned was approximately 8,000ft. Didn't experience any difficulty in abandoning the aircraft. After five seconds I pulled the ripcord and the parachute opened immediately. While descending I noticed a glow through the cloud which at first appeared to be a searchlight, but on breaking cloud appeared to be the burning aircraft, although I had drifted far away from it. I landed near Faulkner Farm about 2 miles from Wisbech. I notified Wing Commander Reid of 409 Squadron immediately by telephone."

Whilst flying at night and in cloud, West was totally reliant on his instruments and it would appear that at least one of them was giving him a false reading. Whilst it is more than possible to fly on a limited number of instruments, it requires the pilot to conduct a mental diagnostic programme to determine which instruments are giving good readings and which are not.

Harry Kirton's Body was found less than 400 yards from the crash and not wearing his parachute, he had died when he had hit the roof of 10 Clarston Avenue in Wisbech. When his parachute was found, it was discovered that it had been deployed and that the rigging lines had been cut on one side. The evidence suggested that once Harry had left the aircraft, he pulled the rip cord too soon and his parachute had become entangled with the aircraft. It was also thought that as he descended, he must have made one last desperate bid for survival by releasing himself from the parachute, once he judged himself to be close enough to the ground, sadly the speeds involved meant there was no chance that this would be successful.

Harry Kirton was from Victoria, British Columbia, where he had worked as an Assistant Post Master and a Clerk in a naval stores. He had joined the RCAF at Edmonton on the 6th January 1942 and had joined 409 Squadron in September 1943. His comrades on 409 Squadron said this of him:

"We extend our deepest condolences to his family and fiancé. Kirt as he was affectionately called, had made innumerable friends during the all too brief time with the squadron and his quiet cheerful personality is deeply missed."

Flying Officer Arthur John Morris AFM
Royal Canadian Air Force

Died 21st March 1944

Arthur John Morris

On this day, 402 Squadron were moving back to Digby from Wellingore. In order to maintain their operational status it was decided to fly two aircraft over first and once they had taken up readiness at Digby, the rest of the squadron would join them. Morris took off at 13:15 hours, as Blue 1 in Spitfire VB AA880. His wingman, Flying Officer Sherk had the call sign Blue 2.

It may have been that Flying Officer Morris thought that it was a fitting occasion for a small aerobatic gesture as they departed. However, impromptu aerobatics are nearly always a bad idea and so it was to prove in this case. Morris and his wingman took off normally and turned to pass back over the squadron's dispersal at low level and high speed. As he did so, he entered a slow roll, a manoeuvre his wingman was clearly not expecting. The two aircraft collided. Morris's fell in a slow spiral, crashing ½ a mile north of Wellingore, killing him instantly. Flying Officer Sherk fared much better and despite his Spitfire's buckled wing, he managed to land at Digby.

The citation for Morris's Air Force Medal read as follows: *'This NCO has shown himself to be energetic and capable and his hard work and interest in his job have contributed materially to the success of the operations carried out at this unit. He has flown 966 hours 55 minutes day and 85 hours 10 minutes night on instructional flying between March 1941 and February 1942. He is cheerful and willing, giving his best at all times'*.

Originally born in Scotland, Arthur had become a Canadian citizen when his parents moved there. He was from Winnipeg, where he had been an elevator operator.

Walter Thomson Börner
German Army

Died 1st February 1946

Following the cessation of hostilities, RAF Wellingore became Prisoner of War Camp 156, Heath Camp. It housed German and Ukrainian prisoners of war, until it finally closed in 1948. Rather than let the prisoners idly bide their time, each was expected to contribute in some respect, some of the inmates were even enrolled into a camp police force to maintain discipline.

Walter Börner had been a Baker by trade, so it was a natural choice to put him to work in the cookhouse. Despite being generally well liked amongst the camp populous, he was not liked by those he worked with in the cookhouse; they suspected him of stealing cigarettes. For people who were on a meagre ration of just fifteen cigarettes a month, this must have seemed a heinous crime. As a result, Walter was cold shouldered to such an extent that he applied for a transfer to other duties.

On the night before his death, the British guards informed him that he was going to be charged with the theft of sugar and rations. The next morning Walter was found by a member of the German Camp Police Force, hanging from a tree. It would seem unlikely that the threat of a charge, to a man already in prison, would have driven him to suicide and indeed the circumstances around his death were very murky indeed. The coroner summed up as follows:

"I do not think I have had the full story somehow, but there is something in the fact that this man was subject to some cold shouldering by his comrades."

A verdict of suicide was recorded. Walter Börner was 45.

Pilot 3 Michael John Desilva Loudon
Royal Air Force

Died 9th November 1949

Michael Loudon died of natural causes in the Royal Air Force Hospital at Nocton Hall. He was 21 years of age. He is recorded at the time as resident at Scraptoft in Leicester.

Chief Technician M J Brophy
Royal Air Force

Died 4th June 1964

Chief Technician Brophy was the passenger in a Citroen being driven by Pilot Officer Christopher Hogg, both were serving at Digby. It is not known at what time the crash occurred, but the car was found at 12:45am with both of its occupants dead. Evidently, it had come off the road and run along a ditch before hitting a small brick bridge which led to a bungalow. The accident had occurred between Algarkirk and Sutterton, with the car apparently travelling towards Digby from the direction of King's Lynn.

Pilot Officer Hogg was married and just two weeks away from the arrival of his fourth child; he would have turned 28 on the day following the accident. He was returned home to York for burial. Chief Technician Brophy was buried with full military honours at Scopwick.

Senior Aircraftman Lewis Eifion Evans
Royal Air Force

Died 8th June 1966

Lewis Evans died of a brain haemorrhage at the Royal infirmary in Sheffield. He had lived at 71 Trenchard Road at Digby and was 23 at the time of his death.

Junior Technician Lawrence Andrew Kenny
Royal Air Force

Died 1st November 1979

Lawrence Kenny died of a traumatic brain injury in Sheffield's Royal Hallamshire Hospital. His injuries had been sustained in an accident, but details of this are not known. He had lived at 107 Trenchard Road at Digby.

The funeral of Junior Technician Kenny

ROYAL AIR FORCE DIGBY
CHURCH OF ST FRANCIS

Senior Aircraftman Kevin Paul Brough
Royal Air Force

7th July 1990

It should have been an enjoyable day at a country fair in Nottinghamshire. Kevin Brough was amongst the crew of an RAF fire engine, from Barkston Heath, that was to be on display there. It was a rainy day, and as the fire engine came down Leadenham Hill on the A 17 it hit a patch of oil and skidded off the road into a tree stump. Kevin who was a front seat passenger was killed instantly.

Kevin was from Staffordshire and an Aston Villa fan. He was a lively character who always had a joke. He had been married for just one year and six days, the line of poetry on his gravestone was one he had given to his wife, just a few days earlier, on their first anniversary.

Identical fire engine to the one in use on the day of the accident

Bibliography

We are indebted to the authors of the following books which assisted and / or enabled us in our research:

609 at War. James Douglas Earnshaw.
Action Stations 2. Bruce Barrymore Halpenny.
Bomber Command Losses (All). W R Chorley
Category Five. Colin Cummings.
Digby Diaries. John Rennison
Fighter Command Losses (all). Norman L R Franks.
Final Landings. Colin Cummings.
High Blue Battle. Dave McIntosh.
High Flight - the Life and poetry of John Gillespie Magee. Roger Cole.
History of 410 Squadron. June 1941 - June 1945. Manitoba Military Museum.
Last Take-off. Colin Cummings.
Lincolnshire Air War. Books 1&2. S Finn.
Lonely Warrior. Jean Offenberg.
Luftwaffe Night Fighter Combat Claims 1939 - 1945. John Foreman.
Metal Birds Two by Ian Blackamore.
Operational Record Books. RAF Digby via National Archives, Kew.
The Battle of Britain Then and Now. Winston G Ramsay.
The Price of Peace. Colin Cummings.
They Shall Grow Not Old. L Allison and H Hayward.
To Fly no more. Colin Cummings.

We are extremely grateful for all the help and support we have received from the Team at the Lima Sector Museum at RAF Digby, without whose valued assistance, this book would have been much more difficult to write.

We are further grateful to the following sources of information: The families, friends and acquaintances of those in the cemetery. All those who have contributed accounts and memories. RAF Digby Museum. The National Archive, Kew. The Lincolnshire Echo. The Library Services and Registrars of Births, Deaths and Marriages and their staff of Lincolnshire and Sheffield Councils. The Station Commander, RAF Digby. Library and Archives, Ottawa, Canada. RAF Museum, Hendon. RAF Air Historical Branch. Commonwealth War Graves Commission. Peter Ford and Rosie Creasey of Metheringham.

The Lima Sector Operations Room Museum RAF Digby

Inside the Sector Operations Room during the war

In the early years of the Second World War the German Luftwaffe pounded Great Britain from the air with the intention of breaking the countries defences and the morale of its people. Achieving both of these aims would make an invasion so much easier.

However, the Royal Air Force was to stand in their way along with the use of radar which was in its infancy and linked with Sector Operations Centres and the Observer Corps (Later the Royal Observer Corps) to guide allied fighters to the enemy.

12 Group, which covered the Midlands and East Anglia, had five sectors - Kirton in Lindsey, Wittering, Duxford, Coltishall and Digby. Digby was the operations HQ for Lima Sector responsible for Central England and as back up support to 11 Group in the South East. Digby had a Sector Operations Room which was within the RAF base initially, although it later moved out to Blankney Hall. The "L" Sector Operations Room on the station at RAF Digby has been faithfully restored to its October 1939 World War Two state as the Sector Airfield Operations Room.

The unofficial opening of the refurbished Operations Room Museum, with seventeen of the wartime operations room members, took place on Thursday 29th May 1997 and was an emotional evening, sparking many memories among the wartime crew including former RAF plotters, signalers, teleprinter operators, wireless operators, RDF tellers and fighter controllers.

One of those wartime signalers present was Charles Mayhew, who as a 19 year old was on duty on 3rd September 1939 and booked in the signal at 1115 hrs which sent Royal Air Force Digby to war. The war declaration signal was given by Charles to the Fighter Controller, who read it out to those on duty and then Charles returned the signal to the Traffic room and kept it. He returned this unique, original signal to the Sector Ops Room Museum on 29th May 1997, where it is on display.

The formal opening was conducted the following evening, on 30th May, with principal guests Air Chief Marshal Sir John Allison AOC-in-C Logistics Command, two further Air Vice Marshals, four Group Captains, four Wing Commanders, two Mayors and several wartime fighter/bomber airmen and local civic dignitaries. The evening was sealed with a magnificent aerial display by a BBMF Spitfire IXX which ended its thunderous sortie with a victory roll through clear blue skies. The Operations Room is set up to represent a typical day during the Battle of Britain. The boards accurately display the pilots and aircraft available from each squadron, their location, the weather and other relevant information. In front of the boards is the plotting table made famous in films like The Battle of Britain and Reach for the Sky. They have a map of the centre of England, the surrounding sea and show incoming raids which were plotted by WAAFs who were controlled by the Sector Control Officer who sat high up overlooking the table and boards. Again all are laid out to represent a day during the Battle.

The museum is operated by volunteers who have researched each squadron and the history and the rooms round the building have been converted into display areas for each squadron and other activities relevant to the time. The Museum is fantastic and well worth a visit. The Museum is open Sundays from First Sunday in May to the first Sunday in October at 11.00 am only for guided tours. There is no need to book but just arrive at the Sports Ground Car Park, opposite the Digby main gate. The tour will depart promptly at 11 am so please arrive in good time. Admission: Free . Group visits can be arranged at other times. Contact is the Visits Co-ordinator at RAF Digby on 01526 327272 or get details on www.airops.freeserve.co.uk/digbyops. Website: Google - Digby Ops Room Museum for several informative web sites.

Above: The Sector Controller's view of the plotting table and the information boards. Below: The Observer Corps spotting incoming enemy aircraft and reporting numbers of aircraft, height, and direction.